R. A. BYRD

THE LIFE OF ST. PAUL

Studies in the Life of St. Paul

BY

ARTHUR GORDNER LEACOCK

"But the Lord said . . . . he is a chosen vessel unto me, to bear my name before the Gentiles, and kings, and the children of Israel." —Acts ix, 15

Fifth Edition

ASSOCIATION PRESS
New York: 124 East 28th Street
London: 47 Paternoster Row, E. C.
1912

Copyright, 1906, by
THE INTERNATIONAL COMMITTEE OF
YOUNG MEN'S CHRISTIAN ASSOCIATIONS

To My
FATHER AND MOTHER

CONTENTS

	PAGE
CHRONOLOGICAL OUTLINE	xi
DIRECTIONS AND SUGGESTIONS	xiii

PART I

INTRODUCTION: THE WORLD AND THE MAN

STUDY
I	The World in St. Paul's Time	3
II	The Birth and Education of St. Paul	10

PART II

THE BEGINNINGS OF THE CHRISTIAN CHURCH

III	The Christian Church: The Descent of the Holy Spirit	19
IV	The Christian Church: First Miracles and First Trials	26
V	The Christian Church: The First Martyr . . .	33

PART III

PAUL THE PERSECUTOR CONVERTED

VI	Paul Persecutes the Church: The Church Spreads beyond Judea	43
VII	The Conversion of Paul	50
VIII	The Gospel is Extended to the Gentiles . . .	57

PART IV

PAUL'S FIRST MISSIONARY JOURNEY

STUDY		PAGE
IX	Missions in Cyprus, Perga, and Pisidian Antioch	67
X	Missions in Iconium, Derbe, and Lystra: The Return to Antioch in Syria	74
XI	A Crisis: Must Gentile Christians Keep the Mosaic Law?	81

PART V

PAUL'S SECOND MISSIONARY JOURNEY

XII	From Antioch to Philippi	91
XIII	From Philippi to Athens	98
XIV	From Athens to Antioch	105

PART VI

PAUL'S THIRD MISSIONARY JOURNEY

XV	From Antioch to Ephesus	115
XVI	From Ephesus to Corinth	122
XVII	Paul's Last Journey to Jerusalem	129

PART VII

PAUL'S ARREST AT JERUSALEM AND VOYAGE TO ROME

XVIII	Paul's Arrest at Jerusalem	139
XIX	Paul Appears before Felix, Festus, and Agrippa: He Appeals to Cæsar	146
XX	Paul is Sent to Rome: His Voyage and Shipwreck	153

PART VIII

PAUL'S IMPRISONMENT AND DEATH AT ROME

STUDY		PAGE
XXI	Two Years in Prison at Rome	163
XXII	Paul's Last Travels, Second Imprisonment, and Death	170

PART IX

THE PERSONALITY AND SERVICE OF ST. PAUL

XXIII Personal Characteristics of St. Paul 179
XXIV Paul's Services to the World 186

Chronological Outline

NOTE: The chronology of Paul's life is extremely difficult and uncertain. The dates given in this outline are substantially those found in Conybeare and Howson's *Life and Epistles of St. Paul*.

A. D.
3   Birth of St. Paul at Tarsus in Cilicia.
16-26   Paul studies with Gamaliel at Jerusalem.
26   Returns to Tarsus.
27-30   Public ministry of Jesus.
30-35   Growth of the Christian Church; the Day of Pentecost; First Miracles and First Trials.
35   Paul comes to Jerusalem; the martyrdom of Stephen.
35-36   Paul persecutes the Church.
36   Conversion of Paul.
36-38   Paul goes from Damascus into Arabia for retirement (three years, Judaically reckoned).
38   Paul flees from Damascus to Jerusalem, and thence to Tarsus.
38-43   Paul at Tarsus.
44   Barnabas brings Paul to Antioch to labor among the Gentile converts.
45   Paul and Barnabas visit Jerusalem to carry relief to the Christians in time of famine.
46-47   Paul at Antioch.
48-49   FIRST MISSIONARY JOURNEY: Paul and Barnabas visit Cyprus, Perga, Antioch in Pisidia, Iconium, Lystra, and Derbe, then return to Antioch in Syria.
50   Paul and Barnabas attend the "Council of Jerusalem," to consider the relation of Gentile converts to the Law of Moses.
51-54   SECOND MISSIONARY JOURNEY: Paul starts from Antioch, and visits Cilicia, Galatia, and Troas in Asia Minor. Crossing into Europe, he goes to Philippi, Thessalonica, Berœa, Athens and Corinth. At Corinth Paul writes *First Thessalonians* (52 A.D.?) and *Second Thessalonians* (53 A.D.?). Leaving Corinth, Paul goes by way of Jerusalem to Antioch, where he writes the *Epistle to the Galatians*.

54-58	THIRD MISSIONARY JOURNEY: Paul leaves Antioch and goes to Ephesus, where he remains three years. Paul writes *First Corinthians* (57 A.D.?) and then goes into Macedonia. In Macedonia he writes *Second Corinthians,* and journeys on to Corinth, where he writes *Romans* (58 A.D.?). Leaving Corinth, he goes by way of Philippi and Miletus to Jerusalem, where he is arrested and sent to Cæsarea.
58-59	Paul in prison in Cæsarea. Has hearings before Felix, Festus, and Agrippa; he appeals to Cæsar.
60	Festus sends Paul to Rome; Paul is shipwrecked at Malta.
61-63	Paul arrives at Rome. While in prison he writes *Philippians, Colossians, Philemon,* and *Ephesians.*
63	Paul is released from prison.
63-65	Paul visits Macedonia, Asia Minor, Crete, and possibly Spain. He writes *First Timothy* and *Titus.*
65	Arrest of Paul, probably at Nicopolis; is taken to Rome and imprisoned; he writes *Second Timothy.*
65	Paul is beheaded by Nero.

Directions and Suggestions

1. These *Studies in the Life of St. Paul* consist of daily lessons, covering a period of twenty-four weeks, a page for each day.
2. Be regular and systematic in your study. Do one lesson each day. Do not fall behind, and then try to cover several lessons at one sitting.
3. Set aside the best ten or fifteen minutes of each day for your study, choosing a time when your mind will be fresh, and when you will not be interrupted.
4. Always begin and close with prayer. Ask that you may have eyes to see, a heart to heed, and a will to obey the Truth.
5. Keep a note-book. In the earlier lessons frequent note-book directions are inserted. Later they are gradually dropped. Form the habit of recording all impressions and questions that come to your mind.
6. The data for the life of St. Paul are derived from two sources: Luke in the Acts of the Apostles gives the leading events in the *outer* life of Paul; the *inner* life must be sought in the Epistles of St. Paul.
7. Because the life of Paul must be pieced together from Acts and from the Epistles, it is not always easy to follow or to remember the narrative. Whenever you lose your grasp upon the order of events, turn back and reread the introductory paragraphs of the lessons last studied. The introductory paragraphs of the several lessons, when read consecutively, form a continuous narrative. Refer also, when necessary, to the chronological outline, page ix.
8. Loosely inserted in this book is an outline map of the Pauline world. This map you are to use, beginning with Study VI, marking upon it with red ink or pencil the places in which the gospel is preached by the apostles.
9. All important variations between the Authorized Version (A.V.) and the Revised Version (R.V.) are noted in these *Studies*. You should have a copy of the Revised New Testament, preferably the American revision.
10. Three books on the life and writings of St. Paul are especially useful: Conybeare and Howson's *Life and Epistles of St. Paul*, New York, is the monumental work on Paul. It is particularly valuable for its descriptions of the countries and cities visited by Paul—their

manners and customs, religious antiquities, government, etc.; it contains also an original translation of the speeches and letters of the Apostle. Canon Farrar's *Life and Work of St. Paul* is rich, imaginative, and rhetorical; it is valuable chiefly for its vivid presentation of important scenes in the life of Paul, and for its clear analysis of his writings. The Rev. James Stalker's *Life of St. Paul* is an inexpensive little manual that should be in the hands of every student of Paul; it is brief, clear, and concise; it traces the growth of Paul's gospel, and reveals the mind and heart of the great Apostle to the Gentiles.

PART I

INTRODUCTION: THE WORLD AND THE MAN

STUDY I.—The World in St. Paul's Time
STUDY II.—The Birth and Education of St. Paul

Study I.—The World in St. Paul's Time
First Day: The Three World-Nations

In the time of St. Paul (3-65 A.D.) there were three nations of world-wide influence—the Romans, the Greeks, and the Jews. The Romans ruled the world: throughout the length and breadth of the Roman Empire their power was felt and feared; the Greeks led the world in intellectual matters, such as language, literature, science, and art: Greek at this time was well-nigh a universal language; the Jews were distinguished for religion: they worshipped the one true God, and had the sacred books of the Old Testament; scattered throughout all lands, they established synagogues, and carried on everywhere the worship of Jehovah.

In view of the spread and influence of these three nations, St. Paul had ideal qualifications as a world-missionary: he was a Roman citizen; he spoke and wrote Greek; and he was by birth a Jew of purest Hebrew stock.

1. Write in your note-book the names of the three world-nations of St. Paul's time, and state in your own words the part each was playing in the life of the age.
2. What was St. Paul's relation to each of these world-nations?
3. Copy in your note-book John 19, verses 19 and 20.
4. Why was the inscription on the cross written in Hebrew, Latin, and Greek?

PRAYER: "Direct us, O Lord, in all our doings with Thy most gracious favor, and further us with Thy continual help, that in all our works, begun, continued, and ended in Thee, we may glorify Thy holy Name, and finally, by Thy mercy, obtain everlasting life; through Christ our Lord." *Amen.*

STUDY I.—The World in St. Paul's Time
SECOND DAY: THE ROMANS

In the time of St. Paul the Romans ruled the world. All of the countries bordering on the Mediterranean, and many other countries inland, were included in the Roman Empire. Spain, Gaul (now France), Italy, Macedonia and Greece, Asia Minor, Syria, Palestine, Egypt, and the parts of Africa west of Egypt were the most important portions of the Empire.

The Romans were great organizers and great builders; they had peculiar skill in governing both themselves and other peoples; they extended their laws and political institutions among the various nations which they conquered; they built excellent roads to connect all parts of their vast Empire. Wherever a Roman citizen went throughout the Roman world, he was entitled to the fullest possible protection. In particular three privileges of the Roman citizen deserve attention:

1. The right of trial by Roman courts.
2. Freedom from scourging, crucifixion, and other degrading punishments.
3. The right of appeal to the Roman Emperor.

St. Paul was a Roman citizen. In Acts 22:28 he says proudly that he is a Roman citizen by birth. This indicates that Paul's father, though a Jew, was likewise a Roman citizen. How Paul's father obtained his Roman citizenship is not known. Possibly he had rendered some important service to the government, in return for which he was made a citizen.

1. Read Acts 22:22-29. Roman citizenship might be obtained in several ways. What two ways are mentioned in the passage just read?
2. Why was the chief captain afraid?

THOUGHT FOR TO-DAY: The Roman Empire helped the spread of Christianity: all the nations of the earth were under one rule; the great military roads were useful to the Christian missionaries in their travels from country to country; Roman citizenship protected certain of the early Christian preachers. As you study history, try to see the hand of God ordering and arranging all things.

Study I.—The World in St. Paul's Time
Third Day: The Greeks

In the time of St. Paul the Greeks led the world in all intellectual matters. They had an exquisite language, capable of expressing the most delicate shades of meaning. Before 350 B.C. the Greeks had produced a rich and extensive literature, had made profound investigations in philosophy, had laid the foundations of the sciences, and had produced matchless works of art.

After 350 B.C. Alexander the Great conquered the greater part of the known world. He planted Greek cities throughout his Empire and spread the Greek language and civilization over the lands of the Mediterranean. After the death of Alexander in 323 B.C., his successors continued his policy of making the world a Greek world. So thoroughly was this work done that long after the Empire of Alexander had passed into the hands of the Romans it kept its Greek character.

In St. Paul's time Greek was well-nigh a universal language. It was spoken in Northern Africa and Egypt, in Palestine, Syria, Asia Minor, Macedonia and Greece. In Rome it was read and spoken by educated Romans and by thousands of foreigners and slaves. In Southern Gaul and even in Spain there were cities in which Greek was spoken. In Palestine the Jews spoke Aramaic, a language closely related to Hebrew, yet Greek was understood generally throughout the land; most of the Jews living outside of Palestine spoke Greek. As early as 250 B.C. the Hebrew Old Testament was translated into Greek, and this Greek version, called the *Septuagint* (because made by seventy rabbis), soon became the popular Bible of Greek-speaking Jews.

1. What was the leading characteristic of the Greeks? See 1 Cor. 1:22 (latter part of the verse) and Acts 17:21.
2. St. Paul spoke Greek. All of his writings are in Greek.
3. The entire New Testament was written in Greek by nine different men, most, if not all, of whom were Jews. Why did they use Greek instead of Aramaic?

PRAYER: "Lord, take my lips and speak through them; take my mind and think through it; take my heart and set it on fire." Amen.

Study I.—The World in St. Paul's Time
Fourth Day: The Jews

The third nation of world-wide extent was the Jewish nation. Strabo, a geographer of the time of Christ, says "it is hard to find a place in the habitable earth that hath not admitted this tribe of men, and is not possessed by it." Jews were to be found everywhere throughout the Roman Empire. This wide dispersion of the Jews was due to several causes. The armies of Assyria, Babylonia, Syria, Egypt, and Rome, had invaded Palestine and had carried off thousands of Jews; thousands of Jews also had gone into foreign lands to engage in trade and commerce.

The Jews were noted for religion; they worshipped the one true God, and they had the sacred books of the Old Testament which contained a record of God's dealing with man from the creation of the world. Wherever the Jews went, they carried their sacred books with them and established synagogues.

The Jews of the Dispersion—that is, those living in foreign lands—were more liberal than those living in Palestine. They had been broadened by contact with the cultivated Greek world. Hebrew, the language of the Old Testament, was a dead language at this time. The Jews of Palestine spoke Aramaic, a dialect related to Hebrew, though very many of them also understood Greek. On the other hand, the Jews of the Dispersion spoke Greek, and used the Septuagint or Greek version of the Old Testament. The Jews of the Dispersion, therefore, were specially qualified to teach the religion of the Old Testament to the Gentile world.

1. Read Acts 2:5-11. From these verses make a list of the countries inhabited by Jews, and notice that this list includes the most important parts of the Roman Empire.
2. Read Acts 15:21. What evidence does this verse furnish?

Thought for to-day: The dispersion of the Jews prepared the way for the Christian Church. The simple religious rites of the Jews attracted to the synagogues many Gentiles who were not satisfied with the idolatrous ceremonies of the pagan temples. The Greek version of the Old Testament could be read by Greeks and by cultivated Romans. The early Christian missionaries were Jews, and as they traveled on their preaching tours they went first to the synagogues of their brethren, the Jews. They were thus able to reach not only Jews, but also such Gentiles as were favorably disposed toward the worship of God.

Study I.—**The World in St. Paul's Time**

Fifth Day: The Jews (Continued)

The Jews, as was learned from the lesson of yesterday, were scattered all over the world. Their chief characteristic was religion. The subject of to-day's lesson, therefore, will be a brief study of the religious history of the Jews.

The world, soon after creation, became wicked. God therefore determined to train up a people in morals and religion. For this end He chose Abraham, and promised him that his children should become a mighty nation. To Abraham and his children God revealed Himself in a peculiarly intimate manner. The descendants of Abraham became in time the great Jewish nation. Moses, under the inspiration of God, gave them laws both for their civil and for their religious life.

The Jewish nation occupied Palestine. They were proud of the favor shown them as the chosen people of God, and were filled with contempt for their heathen neighbors. Nevertheless, they were not faithful to God. They were warned by the prophets and were punished by attacks of foreign armies. Finally, in 722 B.C., ten tribes were carried off by the Assyrians and disappeared from history. About one hundred and twenty-five years later the remaining tribes were carried away by the Babylonians. In 536 B.C. Cyrus the Great allowed them to return to Palestine.

After their return from captivity the Jews became more narrow and exclusive than they had been before. In the days of Jesus the religious life of the nation was at a low ebb. In the eyes of a Jew the all-important thing was to keep the Law of Moses and the oral law based upon it. Jesus sharply rebuked the religious leaders of the Jews, the scribes and Pharisees, for neglecting works of mercy and justice, and for devoting themselves to idle discussion and to the observance of petty and childish rules.

1. Read Jesus' denunciation of the scribes and Pharisees, Matt. 23:13-33.
2. Are there any men to-day who show the spirit of the scribes and Pharisees?

Study I.—The World in St. Paul's Time
Sixth Day: The Morals of the Ancient World

Although the Romans were the political rulers of the world, and the Greeks were the leaders of the world in intellectual culture, and although the Jews were the guardians of the worship of Jehovah, yet each of these world peoples was marred by incredible defects or weakened by vice and crime.

The Romans were avaricious and cruel. They delighted in coarse pleasures, such as wild-beast fights and the combats of gladiators. In early times the Romans lived simply and frugally, but with the growth of the Empire and the increase of wealth, they gave themselves up to luxury, dissipation, and sensuality.

The Greeks had sought their highest good in the study of philosophy; they tried by means of logical proof to establish the doctrine of the immortality of the soul; they sought also by their studies in philosophy to work out a system of rules to govern moral conduct. Yet these efforts, for the most part, were unsuccessful. Many philosophical sects arose, and sober discussion degenerated into senseless wrangling over words and phrases. Meanwhile the moral character of the people as a whole deteriorated. The Greeks were too often fickle and licentious, and many times they misapplied their intellectual arts to make vice attractive.

The Jews were proud and exclusive; they cared more for the observance of the Mosaic law than for mercy and justice. They, too, like the Greeks and the Romans, were often guilty of vice and crime.

St. Paul, in one of his letters, gives an awful picture of the wickedness of his time:

1. The wickedness of the Greek and Roman world. Romans 1:28-32.
2. The wickedness of the Jews. Romans 2:17-24.
3. Read Paul's catalogue of evils in Galatians 5:19-21.

PRAYER: "We pray Thee to compassionate our weakness, O Lord, to guard us in peril, to direct us in doubt, and to save us from falling into sin. From the evil that is around and within us, graciously deliver us. Make the path of duty plain before us, and keep us in it even unto the end." *Amen.*

Study I.—The World in St. Paul's Time
Seventh Day: The Coming of Christianity

The world was in need of a Saviour. Men were weary of their sins, and could find no permanent relief in philosophy or in the systems of morality that had been devised. Gradually the conviction arose that the thing most satisfactory to God was good conduct. Men felt, too, that they must have an ideal life to follow.

The Jews were waiting for the coming of the Messiah. For centuries the Jewish prophets had foretold that the Messiah should be born in the city of David, and that he "should save his people from their sins." Also among the Gentiles at this time there was a widespread belief that a deliverer should appear who would free the world from its sin and wretchedness.

Into this needy and expectant world Jesus Christ came. He was born in Bethlehem of Judea in 5 B.C. His public ministry occupied the years 27-30 A.D., but was confined almost wholly to Palestine. After His death, in 30 A.D., there was need that someone should publish His teachings to the world. At this juncture Paul came forward. Paul organized the scattered teachings of Jesus into a system of religious thought, and then preached Jesus and His plan of salvation throughout the civilized world.

Review of the week's work:

1. What were the three world-nations of St. Paul's time?
2. What was the leading characteristic of each?
3. How did each help in the spread of the Gospel?
4. What was the moral condition of the ancient world?
5. When and where did Christianity arise?
6. What was the relation of St. Paul's work to that of Jesus?

Study II.—The Birth and Education of St. Paul
First Day: The Date of St. Paul's Birth

The exact date of St. Paul's birth is not known. From two verses in the New Testament, however, it is possible to determine approximately the year in which he was born. In the first of these two verses he is called "a young man"; in the second he speaks of himself as "Paul the aged." These verses will be the subject of study to-day.

PAUL THE YOUNG MAN

I. Read Acts 7:58.
   1. Copy this verse in your note-book, substituting for the first "him" the word "Stephen."
   2. Stephen was stoned in 35 A.D.
   3. Therefore St. Paul (or Saul, as he is called here) was a young man in 35 A.D.
   4. The term "young man" is one whose limits are not clearly defined. In general it may be said that a young man is one whose age falls between twenty-one and thirty-five.

PAUL THE AGED

II. Read Philemon, verse 9.
   1. Copy this verse in your note-book.
   2. The Epistle to Philemon was written in 63 A.D.
   3. Therefore St. Paul was an "aged" or old man in 63 A.D.
   4. The term "aged" is also one of considerable latitude. Some men grow old prematurely and may be regarded as old men before their fiftieth year. Others may not seem old until after their seventieth year.

The date of St. Paul's birth must be so fixed that he may be regarded as a young man in 35 A.D., and as an aged man in 63 A.D. The year 3 A.D. has been chosen as a date which meets these requirements. If St. Paul was born in 3 A.D., he was thirty-two years old in 35 A.D. and sixty years old in 63 A.D. This date is also rendered highly probable by reasons which are stated in certain lessons which follow.

PRAYER: "O Lord, give me the grace of Thy Spirit, early to seek out, and evermore earnestly to follow the work which Thou hast appointed for me to do." *Amen.*

Study II.—**The Birth and Education of St. Paul**
Second Day: St. Paul's Birthplace

St. Paul himself twice gives in the New Testament the name of his native city.

1. Read Acts 22:3.
2. Tarsus, the capital of Cilicia, was situated on the Cydnus River, twelve miles from the sea. It was a free city, and possessed certain important rights and privileges; it was also a great center of education, ranking along with Athens and Alexandria. Strabo says that the men of Tarsus were so zealous in the study of philosophy that they surpassed all other men in the study of that subject. Though the city had been Hellenized under the successors of Alexander, yet it was, after all, a place in which the Greek and the Oriental worlds met and blended; it was a Roman city after 94 B.C., yet its inhabitants were free—that is, largely self-governing; the men of Tarsus did not possess Roman citizenship except by special grant. Large numbers of Jews were to be found in the city, attracted thither by the many opportunities for trade and commerce.
3. Read Acts 21:39. Why does Paul in this verse say that he is a citizen "of no mean city."
4. How were each of the three world-nations represented in Tarsus?
5. St. Paul was the first great missionary to the Greek and Roman world. How did the influences of Tarsus fit him specially for this work?

St. Paul was a city-bred man. Most of his work was done in large towns and cities. Jerusalem, Damascus, Antioch, Tarsus, Ephesus, Thessalonica, Corinth, and Rome were the centers of his greatest activity.

"The words of Jesus are redolent of the country and teem with pictures of still beauty or homely toil—the lilies of the field, the sheep following the shepherd, the sower in the furrow, the fishermen drawing their nets. But the language of Paul is impregnated with the atmosphere of the city and alive with the tramp and hurry of the streets. His imagery is borrowed from scenes of human energy and monuments of cultivated life—the soldier in full armor, the athlete in the arena, the building of houses and temples, the triumphal procession of the victorious general."—*Stalker.*

Study II.—The Birth and Education of St. Paul
Third Day: St. Paul's Parents

The names of St. Paul's parents are not known. He was born, however, in a typical Jewish home of the better sort, and was trained in all the traditions held sacred by pious Hebrew parents. St. Paul more than once boasts of his pure Jewish blood.

1. St. Paul's pure Jewish blood: 2 Cor. 11:22.
2. His tribe: Philippians 3:5.
3. His father was a Roman citizen. Acts 22:27 and 28.
4. In Galatians 1:15 Paul alludes, though only incidentally, to his mother.
5. Paul had a married sister living in Jerusalem. Acts 23:16.
6. In Romans 16, verses 7, 11, and 21, Paul sends greeting to certain men whom he designates as "kinsmen." These men may have been either distant relatives or else members of his own tribe, the tribe of Benjamin.

PAUL'S TWO NAMES: Owing to contact with the Greek and Roman world many Jews assumed, in addition to their Hebrew names, a Greek or a Roman name. For example, the Aramaic Hebrew name of Peter was *Cephas (rock)*; the name *Peter* is Greek (*Petros*), and also means *rock*. Peter earlier bore the Hebrew name *Symeon,* while his corresponding Greek name, adopted from similarity of sound, was *Simon*. In the book of Acts, Paul is called Saul until Chapter 13:9; after that point the name Paul is used exclusively. The name *Saul* is a Hebrew word, meaning "asked of God"; the name *Paul* is Roman (*Paulus*), and means "little."

Study II.—The Birth and Education of St. Paul
Fourth Day: Home Life and Training

Jewish children were carefully trained in the history and traditions of their nation. They learned the laws of Moses, and were taught the story of God's constant and loving care for the Jewish people.

1. Moses himself laid down rules for the education of children. Read Deuteronomy 6:4-9.
2. This teaching is re-echoed in the Psalms. See Ps. 78:5-7.
3. Much of this instruction was given by the Jewish mother. From 2 Timothy 3:15 and 1:5 try to picture to yourself the home of the youthful Timothy. Timothy's father, however, was a Greek, while Paul's father was a Jew. Otherwise their homes were similar.
4. Paul's father was a Pharisee. See Acts 23:6. What were the beliefs and practices of the Pharisees?
5. As Paul at his mother's knee heard the Old Testament stories of Abraham, Isaac, and Jacob, of David and the prophets, his heart must have been fired with love for the chosen people and with zeal for the worship of Jehovah. He would also have a feeling of pity, if not of contempt, for his Gentile playmates in the city of Tarsus.

Two languages were probably spoken in St. Paul's home—Aramaic and Greek. Persons so intensely Hebrew as Paul's parents would be likely to speak Aramaic Hebrew in the seclusion of the family circle. At the same time Paul seems to have been familiar with Greek from his boyhood. The style of his speeches and letters is not that of a man who had learned Greek late in life. Greek was the language of Tarsus. Even if Paul did not hear it at home, he would naturally learn it from his playmates in the city.

Lesson Thought: Paul's training at home was a careful study of the Old Testament scriptures. What does Paul himself say of the value of Bible study? Read Second Timothy 3:16 and 17.

Study II.—The Birth and Education of St. Paul
Fifth Day: School Life. Learns a Trade

Concerning Paul's school-days in Tarsus nothing is said in the New Testament either by Luke in the book of Acts or by Paul himself in his own Epistles. It is likely, however, that he attended some school in Tarsus, probably a synagogue school, where he learned to read and write Hebrew, the language of the Old Testament.

It is known that Paul learned a trade. All Jewish boys at this time learned trades. One of the older Rabbis said, "He that teacheth not his son a trade does the same as if he taught him to be a thief." Another Rabbi said, "He that hath a trade in his hand, to what is he like? He is like a vineyard that is fenced."

1. What was St. Paul's trade? See Acts 18:3.
2. At Tarsus a rough cloth called *cilicium* was manufactured from goat's hair. From this tents were made. Possibly Paul's father was a dealer in such tents.
3. While laboring as a missionary, Paul worked at his trade so as not to be dependent on his converts for support:
    (a) At Thessalonica: 1 Thess. 2:9.
    (b) At Corinth: Acts 18:3.
    (c) At Ephesus: Acts 20:34.

THOUGHT FOR TO-DAY: "We commanded you that if any would not work, neither should he eat. For we hear that there are some which walk among you disorderly, working not at all, but are busybodies. Now them that are such we command and exhort by our Lord Jesus Christ that with quietness they work and eat their own bread." St. Paul, *Second Thessalonians* 3:10-12. By precept and by example Paul stood for the dignity of labor. Are you ashamed to work, and do you long for a life of ease, or do you intend to labor and do your part of the world's work? Are you willing also, like Paul, to make your life a life of service for others?

Study II.—**The Birth and Education of St. Paul**
Sixth Day: Paul Studies at Jerusalem

A Jewish boy who was to become a Rabbi usually began to study under a Rabbi, or "doctor of the law," at the age of thirteen. So it may be assumed that Paul went to Jerusalem at that age.

1. In what year did Paul go to Jerusalem to study in a Rabbinical school?
2. What was the name of Paul's teacher? Acts 22:3.
3. For a glimpse of Gamaliel, see Acts 5:34-40.
4. Jewish teachers had a high seat, while their pupils sat on the floor below them. Does Paul anywhere allude to this custom in any passage that you have read?
5. Paul was probably at Jerusalem under Gamaliel for at least ten years.
6. What was Paul taught at Jerusalem? Acts 22:3.

The chief subject of instruction in the Rabbinical schools was the Mosaic law and its interpretation. The Mosaic law is contained in the first five books of the Old Testament. In the course of centuries there had grown up around the laws of Moses a mass of decisions and interpretations, called the *oral law,* which in compass exceeded the original laws on which they were based. Many of these rules were senseless and ridiculous. Jewish students memorized the law and its interpretation. In the schools they spent their time in asking questions, raising objections, and making fine distinctions. While the subjects under discussion were often unworthy, yet such training produced keenness of mind and readiness in debate.

Thought for To-day: Paul was a Pharisee and the son of a Pharisee. He desired the approval of God, and sought to obtain that approval by scrupulously keeping the law of Moses. He tried to be righteous by rule. Are you trying to be righteous merely by obeying the rules of morality, or have you learned, as Paul was soon to learn, that righteousness—that is, being right with God—is obtained by faith in Him?

STUDY II.—The Birth and Education of St. Paul
SEVENTH DAY: PAUL RETURNS TO TARSUS

It is not known exactly how long Paul studied at Jerusalem, nor when he returned to Tarsus. The public ministry of Jesus occupied the years 27 to 30 A.D. Inasmuch as Paul seems not to have seen or heard Jesus, it has been assumed that Paul left Jerusalem shortly before 27 A.D., and that he went to his native city, Tarsus.

The course of events may be summarized as follows: Paul was born in 3 A.D. Until the age of thirteen he lived at Tarsus, learning to read and write Hebrew and Greek, and picking up the simple trade of tent-making. In 16 A.D. he went to Jerusalem, where he studied under Gamaliel for about ten years. In 26 A.D. he returned to Tarsus.

For the next ten years Paul remained at Tarsus. What he was doing during this long sojourn can be only a matter of conjecture. He may have taught as a Rabbi in a synagogue school of the city; he may have worked at his trade; he must surely have been influenced by the life and thought of the cultivated Greek city of Tarsus; he may have attended lectures at the university, and may have taken part in the philosophical discussions that were carried on about him.

Paul shows in his writings and speeches some familiarity with Greek literature, for he quotes from the Cretan poet Epimenides in Titus 1:12, from Aratus or Callimachus in Acts 17:28, and from Menander in 1 Corinthians 15:33. Read these passages, and enter them in your note-book.

THOUGHT FOR TO-DAY: Paul's education in the schools was now complete. His training under Gamaliel at Jerusalem had prepared him for work among the Jews. His knowledge of Greek and his familiarity with Greek life and thought had fitted him for preaching among the Greeks. His Roman citizenship gave him a dignified position in the world, and afforded him protection as he moved about the Roman Empire. But Paul was still an exclusive Pharisee, and was still ignorant of God's plan that he should become a missionary to the despised Gentile nations. Have you ever thought that your plans for your own life may not be God's plans? May not your greatest success and happiness come when you seek to know His will concerning you?

PART II

The Beginnings of the Christian Church

Study III.—The Christian Church: The Descent of the Holy Spirit
Study IV.—The Christian Church: First Miracles and First Trials
Study V.—The Christian Church: The First Martyr

Study III.—The Christian Church: The Descent of the Holy Spirit

First Day: The Promise of the Holy Spirit

As was stated in the last lesson, Paul probably left Jerusalem in 26 A.D., and went back to Tarsus, where he remained for about ten years. He does not again appear in Jerusalem until shortly before the death of the martyr Stephen, in 35 A.D.

While Paul was at Tarsus an event of the profoundest importance took place in Palestine. Jesus Christ went about the land preaching the Gospel of the Kingdom of God. His short but eventful public ministry occupied the years 27 to 30 A.D. Just before His ascension, in 30 A.D., Christ called together His disciples, and promised them that they should receive the gift of the Holy Spirit, and should preach the Gospel to the whole world.

The story of the spread of the Gospel and the growth of the Christian Church is told by Luke in the book of Acts. This narrative will now be the subject of study, inasmuch as when Paul next appears in sacred history he comes forward to engage in the persecution of the Christian Church—the church he was destined later to extend over the whole world.

1. Read Acts 1:1-5.
2. What "former treatise" did the author of Acts write?
3. How large was the Christian Church at the time of Christ's ascension? For evidence on this point read 1 Corinthians 15:3-7.
4. Do you suppose that the disciples understood what was meant by the "baptism of the Holy Spirit" (or Holy Ghost)?
5. Do you understand what the baptism of the Holy Spirit is?

PRAYER: "O God, forasmuch as our strength is in Thee, mercifully grant that Thy Holy Spirit may in all things direct and rule our hearts, through Jesus Christ our Lord." *Amen.*

STUDY III.—**The Christian Church: The Descent of the Holy Spirit**

SECOND DAY: THE PROMISE OF THE HOLY SPIRIT (CONTINUED)

On the day of His ascension Christ again promised His disciples the gift of the Holy Spirit, telling them that they should receive power, and should be His witnesses "unto the uttermost part of the earth." After the ascension of Christ the disciples gathered together at Jerusalem and prayed for the promised gift.

1. Read Acts 1:6-14.
2. Judging from verse 6, what thought seems uppermost in the minds of the disciples?
3. What two important statements are contained in verse 8?
4. Notice the successive steps by which the apostles are to extend the Gospel throughout the world (verse 8, latter part). First they are to preach in Jerusalem, then in the surrounding district of Judea, next in the partly Jewish region of Samaria, and last of all in the Gentile world. This last stage, the extension of the Gospel among the Gentiles, was destined to be St. Paul's work.
5. For what do you think the apostles and women were praying (verse 14)?

"Come, Holy Spirit, heavenly Dove,
　With all Thy quickening powers;
Kindle a flame of sacred love
　In these cold hearts of ours.

"See how we grovel here below,
　Fond of these earthly toys;
Our souls, how heavily they go
　To reach eternal joys.

"Come, Holy Spirit, heavenly Dove,
　With all Thy quickening powers;
Come, shed abroad a Saviour's love,
　And that shall kindle ours."
　　　　　　　　　—*Isaac Watts.*

Study III.—The Christian Church: The Descent of the Holy Spirit

Third Day: The Election of an Apostle to Fill the Place of Judas

While waiting for the coming of the Holy Spirit the eleven apostles chose a successor to Judas Iscariot.

1. Read Acts 1:15-26.
2. In the Authorized Version, verse 18 is rendered, "Now this man purchased a field," etc., while the Revised Version renders it, "Now this man obtained a field," etc. Neither translation is correct. The Greek original means "this man caused a field to be bought." Judas, as narrated in Matt. 27:3-8, was stung with remorse, and brought back the thirty pieces of silver to the chief priests and elders. They in turn got rid of the money by buying the potter's field. Judas was indirectly the cause of the purchase of the field.
3. "Aceldama" (verse 19) is an Aramaic word. Luke is writing for Gentile readers, and therefore translates the word into Greek.
4. Verify the two quotations from the Old Testament in verse 20. They are taken from Psalm 69:25 and Psalm 109:8, respectively.
5. To be an apostle, what qualifications were necessary? See verses 21 and 22.
6. St. Paul did not see or hear Jesus during His ministry on earth. Therefore the enemies of Paul maintained that he was not a true apostle, inasmuch as he had not "companied" with the disciples while Jesus was with them.

PRAYER: "O Heavenly Father, the Author and Fountain of all truth, the bottomless Sea of all understanding, send, we beseech Thee, Thy Holy Spirit into our hearts and lighten our understandings with the beams of Thy heavenly grace. We ask this, O merciful Father, for Thy dear Son, our Saviour Jesus Christ's sake." *Amen.*

STUDY III.—The Christian Church: The Descent of
the Holy Spirit

FOURTH DAY: THE DAY OF PENTECOST

When the Jewish festival called the Pentecost had come, the disciples were all assembled together in one place. Suddenly the Holy Spirit descended upon them, and they began to speak with foreign tongues.

1. Read Acts 2:1-13.
2. The word "Pentecost" is a Greek word, meaning "fiftieth." The day of Pentecost was the fiftieth day after the Passover, and was the second great festival of the Jews. It was a harvest festival, and was celebrated at the close of the grain harvest about the first of May.
3. How many days have elapsed since the ascension of Christ?
4. What do you suppose were the thoughts of the disciples during the period between the Ascension and Pentecost?
5. This gift of tongues (verses 4-8) was not of permanent duration. The disciples were not miraculously enabled to speak foreign languages throughout the rest of their lives. Inasmuch as Greek was already a world language, there was no need of a gift of tongues for missionary purposes. The gift of tongues was an extraordinary phenomenon, designed apparently to arrest the attention of Jews of all nations residing in Jerusalem.
6. Observe from what far-away regions the Jews of verses 5-11 had come. It is possible that later many of them made known in their native cities the story of the wonderful scene they had witnessed at Jerusalem.

THOUGHT FOR TO-DAY: "They were all with one accord in one place." The great blessings of Pentecost came upon the disciples when they were gathered together earnestly seeking in common the gift of the Holy Spirit. Read Matthew 18:19 and 20.

STUDY III.—**The Christian Church: The Descent of the Holy Spirit**

FIFTH DAY: PETER'S SERMON AT PENTECOST

As soon as the report of the descent of the Holy Spirit and the gift of tongues had spread through the city, a multitude gathered about the apostles. In order to account for the strange events of the day, Peter then preached a sermon to the throng. He explained to them that the coming of the Holy Spirit was the fulfilment of prophecy. He also charged them with having killed the Messiah.

1. Read Peter's sermon, Acts 2:14-36, noting especially the character of his argument.
2. The Old Testament prophets foretold the coming of the Messiah and the gift of the Holy Spirit. With these prophecies all Jews were familiar. The early Christian preachers, therefore, endeavored to convince the Jews that the life and death of Jesus fulfilled in every particular the prophecies of the Old Testament, and that consequently He was the promised Messiah.
3. Observe the three forms of address used by Peter: (a) *local*, "Ye men of Judea," (b) *national*, "Ye men of Israel," and (c) *personal*, "Brethren."
4. Explanatory notes and references:
    (a) Verse 15: The third hour of the day was 9 A.M.
    (b) Verses 17-21: This quotation is from Joel 2:28-32, and is taken, not from the Hebrew Old Testament, but from the Septuagint. What was the Septuagint?
    (c) Verses 25-28: See Psalm 16:8-11.
    (d) Verse 34: See Psalm 110, verse 1.
5. In this, as in other speeches and sermons which are preserved in the book of Acts, Luke probably gives only an outline or summary of what was said.

MEMORY VERSE: Memorize Acts 2:17.

Study III.—The Christian Church: The Descent of the Holy Spirit

Sixth Day: The Conversion of Three Thousand Souls

When Peter had finished his sermon, many of the men, deeply affected by the words they had heard, asked what they were to do. Peter bade them repent and be baptized in the name of Jesus Christ. As a result of his sermon and personal exhortation, three thousand souls were converted.

1. Read Acts 2:37-41.
2. Why were Peter's hearers "pricked in their heart" (verse 37)?
3. In verse 39, to whom does Peter refer in the phrase "all that are afar off"? Are they Jews or Gentiles?
4. How large was the Christian Church at the close of the day of Pentecost?
5. The conversion of three thousand souls at Jerusalem was the first step in the fulfilment of a promise made by Christ on the day of His ascension. What was the promise?

PERSONAL THOUGHT: Peter in his sermon endeavored to show that Jesus was the Messiah. He closed with the words, "Let all the house of Israel know assuredly that God hath made Him both Lord and Christ, this Jesus whom ye crucified." At this the Jews were pricked in their hearts. Have you ever been pricked in the heart when thinking of God's goodness to you and of your failure to recognize Him as your Lord and Christ?

PRAYER: "O Lord, who hast mercy upon all, take away from me my sins, and mercifully kindle in me the fire of Thy Holy Spirit. Take away from me the heart of stone, and give me a heart of flesh, a heart to love and adore Thee, a heart to delight in Thee, to follow and to enjoy Thee, for Christ's sake." *Amen.*

STUDY III.—**The Christian Church: The Descent of the Holy Spirit**

SEVENTH DAY: THE FIRST CONVERTS AND THEIR LIFE

Luke, in a few brief sentences, gives a beautiful picture of the joy and gladness that pervaded the apostolic church.

1. Read Acts 2:42-47.
2. What is meant by "the apostles' teaching" (or doctrine) of verse 42?
3. Verse 44: The church at this time was a kind of socialistic community. All things were held in common. St. Chrysostom (345-407 A.D.) calls it "an angelic republic."
4. Verse 46: The Jewish Christians, as may be seen from this verse, still kept up their worship at the temple. To the temple rites they added the simple Christian sacrament of the Lord's Supper, for to this rite the words "breaking bread" refer.
5. Verse 47: "Favor with all the people," that is, with the common people. What was the attitude of the common people toward Jesus? See Mark 12:37. The first opposition to the church came from the highest classes, the priests and Sadducees.

"The life of these early Christians was the poetic childhood of the church in her earliest innocence. It was marked by simplicity, by gladness, by worship, by brotherhood. At home and in their place of meeting their lives were a perpetual prayer, their meals a perpetual love-feast and a perpetual eucharist. In the temple they attended the public services with unanimous zeal. In the first impulse of fraternal joy many sold their possessions to contribute to the common stock. The members of the little community increased daily, and the mass of the people looked on them not only with tolerance, but with admiration."—*Canon Farrar.*

Study IV.—**The Christian Church: First Miracles and First Trials**

First Day: The First Miracle

One day, when Peter and John went up to the temple at the hour of prayer, a beggar, who had been a cripple from birth, asked them for money. Immediately Peter healed the man of his infirmity, whereupon a crowd gathered in amazement about the two apostles.

1. Read Acts 3:1-11.
2. Notice that Peter and John, like the other early Christians, were still loyal to the temple services. See Acts 2:46.
3. What time of day was the "ninth hour" (verse 2)? See p. 23, 4 (a).
4. The "Beautiful Gate" of the temple was made of Corinthian bronze, and far surpassed in value those made of silver and gold.
5. The Greek words in verse 7 which are translated "feet and ankle bones" are technical terms nowhere else used in the New Testament. Is there any reason why Luke, the writer of Acts, should show an accurate and minute knowledge of the human body? See Colossians 4:14.
6. What inference do you draw from verse 8 concerning the religious nature of the lame beggar?
7. "Solomon's porch" (verse 11) was "a great arcade reaching along the whole east side of the temple."
8. Read to-day's lesson again slowly, letting your imagination picture to you the scene of this miracle.

Thought for To-day: The apostles, in healing the lame man, were doing Christ's work. "Have you ever noticed how much of Christ's life was spent in doing kind things—in merely doing kind things? Run over it with that in view, and you will find that He spent a great proportion of His time simply in making people happy, in doing good turns to people."—*Henry Drummond.*

STUDY IV.—The Christian Church: First Miracles and First Trials

SECOND DAY: PETER'S ADDRESS IN SOLOMON'S PORCH

When the crowd had gathered in Solomon's Porch, Peter delivered to them an address. His theme is "Jesus the Messiah." Peter tells his hearers that faith in Jesus has healed the lame man.

1. Read Acts 3:12-26.
2. What points of resemblance do you find between this address and that delivered by Peter on the day of Pentecost?
3. Did Peter in his address at Pentecost say anything about faith? Does he say anything about faith in this address? Is any development of Christian doctrine noticeable?
4. What do you suppose the feelings of the Jews were as they listened to Peter?
5. Were any converted as a result of this address? See Acts 4:4.

THOUGHT FOR THE DAY: "Souls are made sweet not by taking the acid fluids out, but by putting something in—a great love, a new Spirit, the Spirit of Christ. Christ, the Spirit of Christ, interpenetrating ours, sweetens, purifies, transforms all. This only can eradicate what is wrong, work a chemical change, renovate and regenerate, and rehabilitate the inner man. Will-power does not change men. Time does not change men. Christ does. Therefore, 'Let that mind be in you which was in Christ Jesus.'"—*Henry Drummond.*

STUDY IV.—**The Christian Church: First Miracles and First Trials**

THIRD DAY: THE FIRST ARREST OF THE APOSTLES

The priests and the captain of the temple and the Sadducees were grieved because the apostles taught the people the doctrine of the resurrection of Jesus. They therefore seized Peter and John, and put them in prison.

1. Read Acts 4:1-4.
2. The "captain of the temple" (verse 1) was not a military officer. He had charge, however, of the guard of priests and Levites who watched the temple at night.
3. What two reasons had the priests and Sadducees to interfere with the teaching of the apostles? Verse 2.
4. What was the peculiar religious belief of the Sadducees? See Matthew 22:23.
5. Up to this time no opposition had been offered to growth of the Christian body. There was room in the Jewish Church for many sects, such as the Pharisees, the Sadducees, and the Essenes.
6. The priests and the Sadducees formed the Jewish aristocracy. They caused the death of Jesus through fear that His growing power and influence would lead to the end of their own privileges. They now oppose the apostles because they are alarmed at the favor shown the apostles by the common people.
7. How much has the Church grown since the day of Pentecost? See verse 4.

PRAYER: "O God, perfect us in love, that we may conquer all selfishness and hatred of others; fill our hearts with Thy joy, and shed abroad in them Thy peace which passeth understanding; that so those murmurings and disputings to which we are too prone may be overcome. Make us long-suffering and gentle, and thus subdue our hastiness and angry tempers, and grant that we may bring forth the blessed fruits of the Spirit, to Thy praise and glory, through Jesus Christ our Lord." *Amen.*

Study IV.—**The Christian Church: First Miracles and First Trials**

Fourth Day: The Apostles are Brought Before the Sanhedrin

On the day after their arrest, Peter and John were brought before the Sanhedrin, or Jewish Council. When asked by what authority they had done these things, the apostles replied that they had taught and healed in the name of the Lord Jesus. The authorities marveled at their boldness of speech, and after solemnly warning them let them go.

1. Read Acts 4:5-22.
2. The Sanhedrin, before which the apostles were brought for trial, was a Jewish judicial body which sat chiefly to deliberate upon matters pertaining to religion. It consisted of seventy-one members.
3. What three orders composing the Sanhedrin are mentioned in verses 5 and 6? Note that the term "rulers" of verse 5 includes both priests and Sadducees. Many of the priests were Sadducees. (See Acts 5:17.)
4. What promise of aid in such a crisis as this did Jesus make to His disciples? Mark 13:11.
5. A great change has come over the disciples. They are no longer timid and vacillating, as they had been in the days of Jesus, but are strong and courageous. How do you account for this change?

Personal Thought: "They took knowledge of them that they had been with Jesus." Is my own speech, bearing and conduct such that others take knowledge of me that I have been with Jesus? Do I earnestly seek that power which made the disciples so effective?

Prayer: "I need Thee to teach me day by day, according to each day's opportunities and needs. Give me, O my Lord, that purity of conscience which alone can receive, which alone can improve Thy inspirations. My ears are dull so that I cannot hear Thy voice. My eyes are dim so that I cannot see Thy tokens. Thou alone canst quicken my hearing, and purge my sight, and cleanse and renew my heart. Teach me to sit at Thy feet and hear Thy word." *Amen.*

Study IV.—The Christian Church: First Miracles and First Trials

Fifth Day: The Release of the Apostles

The apostles, when released by the Sanhedrin, went back to their brethren, and told them what had taken place. With one accord they all gave thanks to God, and asked Him for increased power to preach the Word. The Holy Spirit then descended mightily upon them.

1. Read Acts 4:23-31.
2. In what place is it likely that the apostles found "their own company" (verse 23) gathered?
3. The prayer contained in verses 24-30 is one of the longest prayers in the New Testament. What other prayer of the apostles have you already found in the book of Acts?
4. From what Psalm are verses 25 and 26 taken?
5. Verse 31: The gift of the Holy Spirit comes after preparation of the heart by prayer. The possession of the Holy Spirit gives joy to the individual life and power to affect the lives of others.

Thought for To-day: Have you ever longed for the joy and the power that proceed from the indwelling of the Holy Spirit? Have you sought by preparation of the heart and by prayer to secure the presence of this Spirit?

Prayer: "Come, O Lord, in much mercy down into my soul, and take possession and dwell there. A homely mansion, I confess, for so glorious a Majesty, but such as Thou art fitting up for the reception of Thee, by holy and fervent desires of Thine own inspiring. Enter then, and adorn, and make it such as Thou canst inhabit, since it is the work of Thy hands. Give me Thine own Self, without which, though Thou shouldst give me all that ever Thou hast made, yet could not my desires be satisfied. Let my soul ever seek Thee, and let me persist in seeking, till I have found, and am in full possession of Thee." *Amen.*

Study IV.—**The Christian Church: First Miracles and First Trials**

Sixth Day: Christian Socialism: Death of Ananias and Sapphira

In these early days the Christians had all things in common. The rich provided for the poor. Many sold their houses and lands, and distributed the money among the needy. Ananias and his wife Sapphira, after selling a possession, brought part of the money to the apostles, but represented that it was the entire sum. On account of this sin both Ananias and Sapphira instantly lost their lives.

1. Read Acts 4:32-37.
2. Were the members of the Christian Church obliged to give their possessions up to the common store? See Acts 5:4.
3. Barnabas (verse 36) seems to have known St. Paul early in life, judging from subsequent passages in Acts. Perhaps in youth Barnabas may have attended the university at Tarsus. Cyprus, the home of Barnabas, is less than fifty miles south of Tarsus. See map, p. 64.
4. Read Acts 5:1-11.
5. In what way does the sin of Ananias and Sapphira exhibit (1) deliberate intention to do wrong, (2) pride, (3) avarice, (4) contempt for God, and (5) disregard of the truth?
6. Why were Ananias and Sapphira punished so severely?
7. The word "church" (verse 11) is here used for the first time in the book of Acts. "Church" in Acts 2:47 (Authorized Version) is an interpolation, and does not appear in the Revised Version.

Prayer: "Almighty God, unto whom all hearts are open, all desires known, and from whom no secrets are hid; cleanse the thoughts of our hearts by the inspiration of Thy Holy Spirit, that we may perfectly love Thee, and worthily magnify Thy Holy Name, through Jesus Christ our Lord." *Amen.*

Study IV.—**The Christian Church: First Miracles and First Trials**

SEVENTH DAY: THE GROWTH OF THE CHURCH

The spiritual power of the apostles and the charity of the Christian believers brought multitudes of converts into the Church; many miracles were wrought by the apostles; and the report of all these things spread about the surrounding district of Judea.

1. Read Acts 5:12-16.
2. In what verses, previously studied, is it stated that the early Christians used to assemble in the temple?
3. How large do you suppose the Church was at this time?
4. Verse 16: The region about Jerusalem, that is, the district of Judea, is now beginning to learn of the work of the apostles. Of what promise is this the fulfilment? See Acts 1:8.
5. The word translated "vexed" is a Greek term often used by ancient Greek medical writers. It is found in only one other passage of the New Testament, namely, in Luke 6:18. What medical or technical words has the physician Luke used already in Acts?
6. Review rapidly the work of this week by reading the introductory paragraph of each lesson.

"Lord, Thou hast promised grace for grace,
To all who daily seek Thy face;
To them who have, Thou givest more
Out of Thy vast, exhaustless store.

"Each step we take but gathers strength
For further progress, till at length,
With ease the highest steeps we gain,
And count the mountains but a plain.

"Help us, O Lord, that we may grow
In grace as Thou dost grace bestow;
And still Thy richer gifts repeat
Till grace in glory is complete."

—*Samuel K. Cox.*

Study V.—**The Christian Church: The First Martyr**
First Day: The Second Arrest of the Apostles

The Church continued to increase in numbers and to grow in favor with the people. In alarm the Sadducees made a second attempt to put down the new faith. They seized the apostles and put them in prison. The apostles, miraculously freed by an angel, returned at once to their work of preaching and teaching, whereupon the Sadducees held them for trial on the charge that they had not obeyed when ordered to cease preaching in the name of Jesus.

1. Read Acts 5:17-26.
2. What three reasons can you assign as the cause of the indignation of the Sadducees (verse 17)?
3. How many of the apostles were arrested? See verse 29.
4. What is meant by the phrase "the words of this life" (verse 20)? Read John 11:25.
5. Verse 21: The "council" was the Sanhedrin; the "senate of the children of Israel" seems to have been an advisory body of elders.
6. From verse 26 what inference do you draw concerning the growth of the Church? See also Acts 2:47; 3:11 and 12; 4:21; and 5:3.
7. Verse 26: "Brought them"—to what place did the officers bring the apostles? See verse 27.

"The same body which had been present at those secret, guilty, tumultuous, illegal meetings in which they handed over the Lord Jesus to their Roman executioners—were again assembled, but now with something of misgiving and terror, to make one supreme effort to stamp out the Galilean heresy."—*Canon Farrar.*

Study V.—The Christian Church: The First Martyr
Second Day: The Trial of the Apostles Before the Sanhedrin: The Speech of Gamaliel

The apostles, when brought to trial, again proclaimed the resurrection of Christ, and charged the Council with his death. Filled with rage, the Sanhedrin planned to slay the apostles, but was checked by the coolness and good sense of the Pharisee, Gamaliel, the teacher of St. Paul. After beating the apostles, they dismissed them with a warning.

1. Read Acts 5:27-42.
2. Notice in verse 28 the contemptuous allusion to Jesus in the words, "this man's blood." In the Talmud, or Jewish commentary on the Old Testament, Jesus is referred to as Peloni, or "so and so."
3. Gamaliel was the most eminent doctor of the law of the times. "His counsel as to the apostles was not from any leaning to Christianity, but from opposition to Sadduceeism in a case where the resurrection was the point at issue, and from seeing the folly of unreasoning bigotry."
4. Nothing more is known concerning Theudas, of verse 36, than is there given. Judas of Galilee (verse 37) headed an insurrection in 6 or 7 A.D., when the Romans were making a census of the Jews for taxation. His watchword was, "We have no Lord or Master but God."
5. Verse 40: The apostles were beaten or scourged. Their punishment did not exceed forty strokes, for that was the number fixed by the Mosaic law. See Deuteronomy 25:3.

Thought for To-day: "They therefore departed from the presence of the council, rejoicing that they were counted worthy to suffer dishonor for the Name." For a reason why Christians should rejoice in tribulations, see St. Paul's words in Romans 5:3-5.

STUDY V.—The Christian Church: The First Martyr
THIRD DAY: SEVEN DEACONS APPOINTED: PAUL COMES TO JERUSALEM

As the growth of the Church continued, the number of needy people dependent on the common funds became so great that the apostles had time for little else save the distribution of food, clothing, and money. In order, therefore, to have more time for preaching and teaching, the apostles appointed seven helpers, or deacons, to take charge of the poor. Paul seems to have come to Jerusalem from Tarsus about this time.

1. Read Acts 6:1-7.
2. The Greek word rendered "Grecian Jews" in the R.V. is incorrectly rendered "Grecians" in the A.V. The Jews of Palestine spoke Aramaic, a language akin to Hebrew, though very many of them also understood Greek. Most of the Jews outside of Palestine spoke Greek. In general the Greek-speaking Jews were more liberal than the Hebrew-speaking Jews. The latter, because they spoke a language closely related to the Hebrew of the Old Testament, felt themselves to be truer to their national ideals than were the Jews who habitually used the tongue of a pagan people.
3. How did it happen that the widows of the Greek Jews were neglected?
4. To "serve tables" is to handle money (verse 2). The Greek word *trapeza* (*table*) also means *bank*, when applied to the tables of money lenders.
5. Verse 5: The seven men named in this verse all have Greek names. Of the seven, only Stephen and Philip are subsequently mentioned in the New Testament.
6. Paul probably came to Jerusalem about this time, since he was present at the stoning of Stephen, which took place not long after the events of to-day's lesson.
7. What special accessions to the ranks of the disciples were there at this time? See verse 7.

THOUGHT FOR THE DAY: Stephen was a man "full of faith and of the Holy Ghost." The heart that is ready may through *faith* receive the Holy Spirit. Read carefully St. Paul's prayer for the Ephesians, in Ephesians 3:14-21, dwelling especially on verse 17.

STUDY V.—**The Christian Church: The First Martyr**
FOURTH DAY: STEPHEN ARRAIGNED BEFORE THE SANHEDRIN

Stephen, the most able and energetic of the seven men appointed to distribute the relief funds, soon joined in debate with the foreign Jews, and proved too much for them in argument. Whereupon they brought him before the Sanhedrin, after preparing lying witnesses, in order to convict him of blasphemy and put him to death.

1. Read Acts 6:8-15.
2. Verse 8: "Six good things about Stephen:
   (1) Full of faith (verse 5).
   (2) Full of the Holy Ghost (v. 5).
   (3) Full of power (v. 8).
   (4) Full of irresistible energy and power (v. 10).
   (5) Full of sunshine (v. 15).
   (6) An intrepid witness for God (chapter 7)."
   —*D. L. Moody.*
3. The Libertines (verse 9) were probably the children of Jews who had been carried to Rome and then freed at a later time. Cyrene was a Greek city of north Africa, Alexandria a Greek city of Egypt. Asia in the book of Acts is always the province of proconsular Asia. Locate all these cities and regions on the map.
4. It is altogether likely that Paul at this time attended the synagogue of the Cilicians (verse 9). He would therefore hear the arguments of Stephen.
5. They "set up false witnesses" (verse 13). Compare also Matt. 26:59-61 and Mark 14:57-59.
6. It is not exactly clear what the teachings of Stephen were. Apparently he taught that the Laws of Moses were not essential to salvation—that man could be approved of God and justified in His sight without obedience to the oral or written law.
7. Verse 15: "Three men in the Bible whose faces shone: Moses, Jesus, and Stephen."—*Moody.*

PRAYER: "Lord, make us to resemble even here the heavenly kingdom, through mutual love, where all hatred is quite banished, and all is full of love, and, consequently, full of joy and gladness." Amen.

Study V.—The Christian Church: The First Martyr
Fifth Day: Stephen's Defense Before the Sanhedrin

Stephen, when arraigned before the council, delivered the speech or sermon contained in the seventh chapter of Acts. This sermon consists of two parts, (1) a historical part (verses 2-47), and (2) a doctrinal part with personal application to his hearers (verses 48-53).

1. Read the first part of Stephen's address: Acts 7:1-47.
2. These verses are an excellent epitome of Jewish history from the call of Abraham down to the building of Solomon's Temple. Verses 2-16 are an abridgment of the contents of the book of Genesis; verses 17-41 are an abridgment of the first thirty-two chapters of Exodus; while verses 42-47 constitute in briefest possible form a synopsis of the narrative contained in Exodus (chapters 33-40), Leviticus, Numbers, Deuteronomy, Joshua, Judges, Ruth, 1 and 2 Samuel, and 1 Kings 1-8.
3. The verses you have read to-day should help you to understand better the position of the Jews: their intense national pride; their knowledge of God's constant kindness to them in the past; their feeling of superiority over their less-favored neighbors; and their devotion to their own peculiar rites and ceremonies.

PRAYER: "Help me, O Lord, that I may not, like the children of Israel of old, be blind to Thy leading. Grant that I may see how Thou orderest all things for my good, and enable me to trust Thee, and love Thee, and serve Thee day by day." *Amen.*

Study V.—The Christian Church: The First Martyr

Sixth Day: Stephen's Defense Before the Sanhedrin (Continued)

After Stephen had reviewed the history of the Jews from the call of Abraham down to the building of Solomon's Temple, he passed, by a rapid transition, to the statement that God dwells not in temples made by hands, but in the temple of the human heart. Failure to recognize this had led the Jews to resist the Holy Ghost and slay Jesus, the Just One.

1. Read the second part of Stephen's address: Acts 7:48-53.
2. Does Stephen answer at all the false charges brought against him in chapter 6, verses 13 and 14?
3. What three specific charges does Stephen bring against his hearers in verses 51 to 53 of chapter 7?
4. Can you prove, from any passages of Acts already studied, the truth of these charges made by Stephen against the Jews?
5. With verses 48 and 49 compare what Paul says in Acts 17:24 and 25.

Thought for To-day: "Know ye not that ye are the temple of God and that the Spirit of God dwelleth in you? If any man defile the temple of God, him shall God destroy; for the temple of God is holy, which temple ye are." St. Paul, *First Epistle to the Corinthians*, 3:16 and 17.

Prayer: "Open wide the window of our spirits, and fill us full of light; open wide the door of our hearts, that we may receive and entertain Thee with all our powers of adoration and love." *Amen.*

STUDY V.—**The Christian Church: The First Martyr**

SEVENTH DAY: THE MURDER OF STEPHEN: PAUL APPROVES THE DEED

The Jews, cut to the heart by the words of Stephen, rushed upon him, dragged him outside the city, and stoned him to death. Paul was present, and took an approving part, at least, in the death of Stephen.

1. Read Acts 7:54-60.
2. What three reasons did you discover in yesterday's lesson for the frenzy of the Jews against Stephen?
3. Verse 38: In stoning Stephen outside the city the Jews were obeying the Mosaic law. See Leviticus 24:13-16. But which one of the Ten Commandments did they break?
4. The witnesses were obliged to cast the first stones, hence they removed their outer garments. See Deuteronomy 17:6 and 7.
5. *A young man whose name was Saul.* This is the first mention of Paul in the book of Acts. He is here called by his Hebrew name Saul. The name Paul is not introduced until Acts 13:9.
   (a) How did it happen that Paul had both a Hebrew and a Roman name?
   (b) In what year was Stephen stoned?
   (c) How old was Paul at this time?
6. What part did Paul take in the death of Stephen? Read Acts 8:1 (first sentence), and Acts 22:20.
7. Why did Paul consent to his death?
8. Read slowly Acts 7:54-60, and 8:1 (first sentence), and let your imagination picture to you the death of the first martyr and the approving part taken by Paul.

PRAYER: "Living or dying, Lord, I would be Thine; keep me Thine own forever, and draw me day by day nearer to Thyself, until I be wholly filled with Thy love, and fitted to behold Thee, face to face." *Amen.*

PART III

PAUL THE PERSECUTOR CONVERTED

STUDY VI.—Paul Persecutes the Church: The Church Spreads Beyond Judea
STUDY VII.—The Conversion of Paul
STUDY VIII.—The Gospel is Extended to the Gentiles

Study VI.—Paul Persecutes the Church: The Church Spreads Beyond Judea

First Day: Paul the Persecutor

Paul, believing that the followers of Jesus had embraced a dangerous heresy, and were likely to bring into contempt the laws of Moses and the services of the Temple, now took up with vigor the persecution of the Church. He thought he could stamp out the growing sect. So severe was the persecution that the Church was scattered throughout Judea and Samaria. The very means taken to suppress the Church only resulted in its wider diffusion.

1. Read Acts 8:1-3.
2. From the standpoint of Paul's training and education, what reason or reasons were there why he should persecute the Church?
3. In his speech before Agrippa (Acts 26:10), Paul says of this persecution, "and many of the saints did I shut up in prison, having received authority from the chief priests; and when they were put to death I gave my vote against them" (Revised Version). From the last clause of the quotation it is inferred by some that Paul was a member of the Sanhedrin.
4. If Paul was a member of the Sanhedrin, in order to meet the requirements for admission to that body he must have been at least thirty years old, and must have been married. According to the dates given in an earlier lesson of this book, Paul was thirty-two years old at this time. Paul nowhere mentions his wife; in fact, he distinctly says in 1 Cor. 7:8 that he has no wife. First Corinthians was written about 57 A.D. If Paul was a member of the Sanhedrin, and was married, it is likely that his wife died before 57 A.D.
5. Paul by his persecution was spreading the Church. "Saul, the persecutor, was doing by opposite means the same work as Paul the Apostle."

PRAYER: "O Lord, forgive what I have been, sanctify what I am; and order what I shall be." *Amen.*

Study VI.—Paul Persecutes the Church: The Church Spreads Beyond Judea

Second Day: Paul the Persecutor (Continued)

In his letters and speeches Paul speaks with deepest regret of his persecution of the Christians. Several of these passages are cited below, and form the subject of to-day's lesson.

1. Paul's work of persecution was conscientiously done: Acts 26:9.
2. It was done with vehemence and vigor: Acts 26:10-11; Galatians 1:13; Philippians 3:6.
3. It was done through ignorance and unbelief: 1 Timothy 1:12 and 13.
4. Jesus Himself foretold such persecution: John 16:2.

"Terrible were the scenes which ensued. He flew from synagogue to synagogue, and from house to house, dragging forth men and women, who were cast into prison and punished. Some appear to have been put to death, and, darkest trait of all, others were compelled to blaspheme the name of the Saviour."

"It may seem too venturesome to call this the last stage of Paul's unconscious preparation for his apostolic career. But so indeed it was. In entering on the career of a persecutor he was going on straight in the line of the creed in which he had been brought up; and this was its reduction to an absurdity. Besides, through the gracious working of Him whose highest glory is out of evil still to bring forth good, there sprang out of these sad doings in the mind of Paul an intensity of humility, a willingness to serve even the least of the brethren of those whom he had abused, and a zeal to redeem lost time by the parsimonious use of what was left, which became permanent spurs to action in his subsequent career."—*Stalker*.

Study VI.—Paul Persecutes the Church: The Church Spreads Beyond Judea

Third Day: The Church Scattered by Persecution

Many times in the history of the Church its enemies have endeavored to kill it by persecution. Such attempts have usually resulted in spreading the Church over a wider area, and in diffusing the doctrines of Christianity among a greater mass of men. The persecution that arose after the death of Stephen had this same result.

1. Read Acts 8:1 and 4, noticing particularly the regions to which the Christians flee for safety.
2. It is Luke's practice to unfold in methodical fashion the orderly growth of the Church. First he makes the general statement contained in chapter 8, verses 1 and 4, concerning the dispersion of the Christians. Next he proceeds to name specific towns and cities where the Gospel was preached.
3. Loosely inserted in this book is an outline map of the Pauline World. As stated in the introduction (p. xiii), this map is to be used in tracing the growth of the Church and in showing the part that St. Paul took in that development. If from this time on you mark with a cross (×) by means of red ink or a red pencil all the places in which Paul or the apostles preach the Gospel, you will be able to follow in an interesting manner the extension of the Church through the Roman Empire.
4. The Gospel has now been thoroughly preached in Jerusalem: See Acts 5:28. Mark Jerusalem with a cross.
5. Believers are now scattered throughout the regions of Judea and Samaria. They are telling the Gospel story and are preparing the way for the work of the apostles. Place two or three crosses in Judea and in Samaria.
6. The Gospel has now spread from Jerusalem through Judea and Samaria. Of what promise of Christ is this the fulfilment? Acts 1:8.

Study VI.—Paul Persecutes the Church: The Church Spreads Beyond Judea

Fourth Day: Philip Preaches in Samaria

Through the influence of Christian refugees from Jerusalem, and through the preaching of Philip, the Gospel now spreads beyond Judea into the region of Samaria. Samaria was a district inhabited by a mixed people, partly of Eastern and partly of Hebrew origin. Upon the Samaritans the Jews themselves looked with scorn and contempt. Therefore the extension of the Gospel to the Samaritans was an important event, inasmuch as it was the first step away from Jewish exclusiveness in the direction of the Gentiles.

1. Read Acts 8:5-8.
2. Who was Philip, mentioned in verse 5? See Acts 6:5.
3. Samaria lay north of Judea (see map, p. 64). It was occupied in ancient times by ten tribes of the Hebrew nation. Part of this population was carried off in 722 B.C. by Sargon, king of Assyria. Later the kings of Assyria brought thousands of men from Arabia and from the region of the Tigris and Euphrates, and settled them in Samaria. These newcomers intermarried with the Jews who had remained in the land, and produced the mixed race known as the Samaritans. The Samaritans claimed kinship with the Jews, and maintained a rival Temple of Jehovah on Mount Gerizim. The Jews regarded them as little better than Gentiles.
4. For a reference in the Gospels to the relations existing between Jews and Samaritans, see John 4:9.
5. Samaria was prepared for the preaching of Philip:
    (a) By the labors of Jesus. See John 4:39-42.
    (b) By Christian refugees. See Acts 8:1 and 4.
6. The Samaritans had the Hebrew Scriptures, and kept the Law of Moses. On the other hand, they were partly of Jewish and partly of Gentile blood. They were one of the links between Jews and Gentiles.
7. Mark the city of Samaria with a cross upon your outline map.

Study VI.—**Paul Persecutes the Church: The Church Spreads Beyond Judea**

Fifth Day: Philip and Simon the Sorcerer

While Philip was preaching in Samaria, the apostles Peter and John came down from Jerusalem and laid their hands upon the Samaritan converts, who immediately received the gift of the Holy Spirit. Among these converts was a sorcerer named Simon. Seeing what was done, and wishing to use this gift for improper purposes, Simon brought money and offered it to the apostles that he might obtain the power to communicate the Holy Spirit. For this covetous and presumptuous deed he was sternly rebuked.

1. Read Acts 8:9-25.
2. Verse 9: It is not clear by what means Simon performed his wonders, whether by sleight-of-hand, clairvoyance, or hypnotism.
3. Why did the apostles at Jerusalem send Peter and John down into Samaria?
4. Simon's sin lay in the motive that prompted him to secure the power of communicating the Holy Spirit, and also in the thought that the Holy Spirit could be bought for money. He wanted the Holy Spirit not for his own spiritual growth and advancement, but to use as a wonder and as a means by which he might astonish the people.
5. What does the word *simony* mean?
6. Verse 25: The Gospel has spread still farther about Samaria. Place one or two additional crosses in the region of Samaria on your outline map.

Thought for the Day: God will not let us bargain with Him for righteousness or for His approval. Have you ever vowed that if God would grant you the desire of your heart you would serve Him? Do you not already owe Him the loving service of your life in return for what He has done and is doing for you?

Study VI.—**Paul Persecutes the Church: The Church Spreads Beyond Judea**

Sixth Day: Philip and the Ethiopian Eunuch

While Peter and John were preaching in Samaria, Philip was sent by an angel to meet the chamberlain or treasurer of Candace, queen of Ethiopia. This chamberlain had been at Jerusalem to worship, and was now on his way back to Africa. Taught by Philip, the eunuch confessed Christ, and was baptized.

1. Read Acts 8:26-40.
2. Verse 26: There were two roads from Jerusalem to Gaza. The northern road led to Ascalon, then down the coast to Gaza; the southern road led past Hebron, through desert country, to Gaza.
3. Ethiopia was a country of uncertain extent lying south of Egypt, between the Nile and the Red Sea. Ethiopia and the Ethiopians are frequently mentioned in the Old Testament. After Egypt had been made a Greek kingdom by Alexander and his successors, Greek literature penetrated into Ethiopia. Thither also seems to have gone the Greek version of the Old Testament, for from it the eunuch was reading.
4. Verses 32 and 33: These verses are quoted from the Septuagint or Greek version of the Old Testament.
5. To whom does the prophecy in verses 32 and 33 refer?
6. Tradition says that the eunuch became the founder of the Christian Church in Ethiopia. For a prophecy regarding Ethiopia see Psalm 68, latter part of verse 31.
7. In your outline map mark with crosses the cities of Azotus and Cæsarea.
8. Philip is not mentioned again in Acts until verse 8 of chapter 21, when Paul and his party were entertained by him at Cæsarea, twenty years after the events of to-day's lesson.

Thought for To-day: Philip obeyed God's messenger and became a great means of good to the Ethiopian chamberlain. Are you ready always to obey the promptings of God's Spirit for service among those whom you may influence?

Study VI.—Paul Persecutes the Church: The Church Spreads Beyond Judea

Seventh Day: Review Lesson

You have now finished the *Studies* which precede the conversion of Paul. Before going on it will be helpful to review briefly the work of the past six weeks.

1. What were the three world-nations in St. Paul's time?
2. How did each nation help prepare the way for the spread of Christianity?
3. What was the moral condition of the world at this time?
4. When and where did Christianity rise?
5. When and where was St. Paul born?
6. How was he qualified to work and preach in a world that was at the same time Greek, Roman, and Jewish?
7. What did Paul study at Jerusalem?
8. Did Paul see Jesus?
9. What promise and what prophecy did Jesus make to His disciples on the day of His ascension?
10. What were some of the results of the descent of the Holy Spirit?
11. What causes led to the death of Stephen?
12. Trace the spread of Christianity outward from Jerusalem.
13. What has been Paul's attitude toward the Christian Church, and why has he taken this attitude?

Prayer: "Almighty God, our heavenly Father, without whose help labor is useless, without whose light search is vain, invigorate my studies, and direct my inquiries, that I may by due diligence and right discernment establish myself and others in Thy holy faith. Let me not linger in ignorance, but enlighten and support me, for the sake of Jesus Christ our Lord." *Amen.*

Study VII.—The Conversion of Paul
First Day: Paul on the Road to Damascus

Paul hoped to stamp out the new faith, but his vigorous persecution of the Christians only resulted in scattering them throughout Judea, Samaria and the regions beyond. Enraged because his efforts to destroy had operated to spread the new belief, Paul secured letters from the high priest, and set out for Damascus to arrest all Christians whom he might find in that city. As Paul drew near to Damascus a voice from heaven spoke to him, he fell to the ground, and was smitten with blindness. His companions then led him into the city.

1. Read Acts 9:1-9.
2. What do you suppose were Paul's thoughts while on the way to Damascus?
3. Verse 5: With this verse compare Acts 26:14, and notice the statement, "It is hard for thee to kick against the goad." This is a metaphor derived, like so many of the figures and illustrations of Jesus, from the scenes of country life. The figure is that of an ox kicking against the goad. It was a proverbial expression, signifying "to offer vain resistance." This verse is of the utmost importance for understanding Paul's condition of heart at this time. He was trying to be righteous by obeying the Mosaic law. His zeal for the Law caused him to persecute the Christians. He may have seen in the daily life and character of the Christians whom he persecuted that which led him to doubt and question his own course. Yet to quiet the prick of conscience he threw himself heart and soul into the work of making havoc of the Church.
4. What were some of Paul's thoughts during the next three days?

Thought for the Day: During his three days of blindness Paul's whole previous life "fell down in fragments at his feet." He had sought to gain the favor of God by scrupulous obedience to the Law. His life had been consistent but misdirected. Are you trying to secure the favor of God by rules and laws of your own making, rather than by accepting Him by faith as your Saviour?

Study VII.—**The Conversion of Paul**

Second Day: The Conversion of Paul

While Paul, fasting and in darkness, was thinking and praying over the strange experience that had befallen him, he had a vision in which a disciple named Ananias came to him and restored his sight. Simultaneously, Ananias was prepared by means of a vision to visit Paul. Accordingly, Ananias went to Paul, and laid his hands upon him. At once Paul received his sight and was filled with the Holy Ghost. He then received Christian baptism, and remained some days with the disciples.

1. Read Acts 9:10-19.
2. For what was Paul praying (verse 11)?
3. Judging from the narrative, what was the condition of Paul's heart at this time?
4. Verse 15: In this verse the three world-peoples of St. Paul's time are named:
   (a) Romans: The "Kings" before whom Paul appeared were Nero and King Agrippa, also remotely, the rulers Felix and Festus, who represented the Roman Emperor in the East.
   (b) Greeks: The word "Gentile" is often used as a designation of the Greek pagan world.
   (c) Jews: The "children of Israel."
5. "Then was Paul certain days with the disciples which were at Damascus." The expression rendered "certain days" may be translated "some days." It is found also in Acts 10:48; 15:36; 16:12; 24:24; and 25:13. In all these passages the time indicated is brief.

> "The Shepherd sought His sheep,
>   The Father sought His child;
> He followed me o'er vale and hill,
>   O'er deserts waste and wild;
> He found me nigh to death,
>   Famished, and faint, and lone;
> He bound me with the bands of love,
>   He saved the wandering one."
>
> *—Horatius Bonar.*

Study VII.—**The Conversion of Paul**

Third Day: Paul Preaches in Damascus

During the short time that Paul tarried in Damascus he visited the synagogues and preached Christ. In the synagogues were many devout Jews, probably, also, some Greek proselytes. The Jews of Damascus seem to have been less fanatical than the Jews of Jerusalem; consequently Paul, at first, was able to gain a hearing.

1. Read Acts 9:20-22.
2. Verse 21: From this verse it would seem that the synagogue congregations of Damascus were not greatly disturbed by the preaching of Christian doctrine.
   (a) Were the Jews outside of Palestine more or less liberal than the Jews of Palestine?
   (b) How do you account for this difference?
3. Damascus is perhaps the oldest city in the world. It early became the most important city of Syria. Its importance was due to its situation and to the wealth which it accumulated. For the commercial importance of Damascus, see Ezekiel 27:16 and 18.
4. Mark Damascus with a cross on your outline map.
5. Verse 22: Paul, the well-trained Rabbi, skilled in all the subtle arguments of the Pharisees, now brings all his extensive knowledge of the Old Testament and its traditions to prove that Jesus is the Messiah.

Thought for the Day: "Straightway he preached Christ." Paul is remarkable for his intensity, vigor, and promptness of action. A verse in one of his letters to Timothy may be said to be his motto: "Preach the word; be instant in season, out of season, reprove, rebuke, exhort with all long-suffering and doctrine." 2 *Tim.* 4:2.

Study VII.—The Conversion of Paul
Fourth Day: Paul Retires to Arabia

After preaching a few days in Damascus, Paul retired to Arabia for rest and meditation. How long he remained in Arabia is not entirely certain, yet his sojourn was not over three years.

1. Read Galatians 1:15-17.
2. Arabia, a vast region bounded on the north by Palestine and Syria, on the east by the Euphrates and the Persian Gulf, on the south by the Arabian Sea and the strait of Bab-el-Mandeb, and on the west by the Red Sea and Egypt. See map, p. 64. Notice that a portion of Arabia lies east of Damascus.
3. Can you think of any reasons why Paul should withdraw to Arabia?
4. What leader of Old Testament times spent forty years of retirement in Arabia? See Acts 7:29 and 30.
5. Paul retired to Arabia probably because he wished to gain time for rest and reflection. The whole current of his life had been changed. He wanted time to think over the past, to realize the significance of the present, and to prepare for his work in the future. It is likely that during this period of retirement his conception of the divine plan of salvation by faith took form —a conception which he later set forth fully in his letter to the Romans. Paul had sought the favor of God by excessive zeal for the Law of Moses and the traditions of the fathers. Now he had found that God's favor and approval were secured by repentance and by faith in Jesus Christ. Read Romans 3:19-28.

Thought for To-day: Goethe says: "Talent develops itself in solitude; character in the stream of life." St. Paul's retirement into Arabia prepared him for the severe toils and labors that awaited him in the world; and these hardships, when they came, all contributed to fashion his character into that strength which excites our admiration.

Study VII.—**The Conversion of Paul**

Fifth Day: Paul Returns to Damascus: His Flight to Jerusalem

After his period of retirement in Arabia, Paul returned to Damascus, and took up again with increased power his work in the synagogues. Learning of a plot of the Jews to kill him, Paul escaped from Damascus, and went to Jerusalem, where he remained a short time with the disciples.

1. Read Acts 9:23-28.
2. The "many days" of verse 23 constitute the time from Paul's conversion to his escape to Jerusalem, and include his sojourn in Arabia. How long a space of time was this? Gal. 1:18.
3. The "three years" of Gal. 1:18 may be actually only a little over a year. According to Jewish methods of reckoning, from a point near the end of one year to a point shortly after the beginning of the second year following was a space of three years.
4. Paul himself tells how the Jews lay in wait for him at Damascus: 2 Cor. 11:32, 33.
5. Why did the Jews seek to kill Paul?
6. "Aretas the King," mentioned in 2 Cor. 11:32, was the king of Arabia. Damascus was a city of the Roman province of Syria. Damascene coins of Augustus and Tiberius, and afterward of Nero and other emperors, have been found, but none for the reign of Caligula. Therefore, it seems probable that during his reign (37-41 A.D.) some change in the government took place. From 2 Cor. 11:32 it appears that Damascus belonged to Arabia at the time when Paul made his escape. Paul's escape, therefore, must have taken place at some time within the years 37-41 A.D.
7. Why was Barnabas the one to befriend Paul at Jerusalem? See p. 31, section 3.
8. How many apostles were in Jerusalem at this time? See Galatians 1:18-20.
9. How long did Paul stay at Jerusalem?

Thought for the Day: Observe with what power Paul does his work after his retirement in Arabia. Do you personally know the value of the quiet hour for self-examination and prayer as a preparation for service?

STUDY VII.—**The Conversion of Paul**

SIXTH DAY: PAUL PREACHES AT JERUSALEM: HIS FLIGHT TO TARSUS

During his stay of two weeks at Jerusalem, Paul spoke and taught boldly in the name of the Lord Jesus. So vigorous was his preaching that the Jews were moved with anger, and sought to kill him, but Paul escaped and went to Tarsus.

1. Read Acts 9:29 and 30.
2. Verse 29: The word translated "Grecian Jews" in the R.V. is incorrectly rendered "Grecians" in the A.V.
3. Paul probably preached in the very synagogues in which Stephen had been so active. See Acts 6:9.
4. Why did the Greek Jews plan to slay Paul?
5. During this sojourn of a fortnight in Jerusalem, Paul had a vision in which his mission to the Gentiles was stated to him clearly.
   (a) Read Acts 22:17-21.
   (b) Had Paul known before this time that he should be an apostle to the Gentiles? See Acts 22:12-15.
6. Verse 29: Paul now begins to suffer the trials that were his promised lot. See Acts 9:16.

LESSON THOUGHT: The opposition that Paul met in Jerusalem must have caused him deep sorrow. He had hoped, undoubtedly, to undo some of the wrong he had done to the Christian Church in that city. But God's plans are wider than the plans of men. It was His design that Paul should preach to the world, not to the provincial city of Jerusalem; hence came the command: "Depart, for I will send thee far hence unto the Gentiles."

Study VII.—The Conversion of Paul
Seventh Day: Review Lesson

The apostles have now spread the Gospel over Judea and Samaria. The next step is to extend it to the Gentiles. Before passing to this new subject, Luke inserts in his narrative a brief summary of the growth of the Church.

1. Read Acts 9:31.
2. Such summaries as the one just read are placed by Luke at the end of distinct periods in the growth of the Church. What ones have you noticed already?
3. Read rapidly in review the introductory paragraphs of the lessons of this Study (VII), pp. 50-56.
4. Paul is now at Tarsus. By his birth of Jewish parents in a Greek city, and by his possession of Roman citizenship, he is ideally qualified to labor anywhere in the world. By his training at Jerusalem, his conversion, his meditation in Arabia, and by his preaching at Damascus and Jerusalem, he has been fitted to labor as a Christian missionary. He is now at Tarsus awaiting orders.
5. While Paul was at Tarsus he may have founded some Christian churches in Cilicia. In Acts 15:23, churches of Cilicia are mentioned, though no account is given of their planting.
6. Mark Tarsus with a cross on your outline map.
7. Study your outline map carefully, noticing particularly all towns or cities in which the Gospel has been preached up to this point in the narrative.

PRAYER: "O God, who through the preaching of the blessed Apostle Saint Paul, hast caused the light of the Gospel to shine throughout the world; grant, we beseech Thee, that we, having his wonderful conversion in remembrance, may show forth our thankfulness unto Thee for the same, by following the holy doctrine which he taught; through Jesus Christ our Lord." *Amen.*

Study VIII.—The Gospel is Extended to the Gentiles
First Day: Peter at Lydda and Joppa

While Paul sojourned at Tarsus, the Church was prepared for his labors by a step of the greatest importance. That step was the extension of the Gospel to the Gentiles, and was due to the work of Peter while engaged in a preaching tour of Palestine.

1. Read Acts 9:32-43.
2. The phrase "throughout all quarters" (or "parts") seems to indicate that Peter had been traveling about, in order to preach and to strengthen the churches. When Paul visited Jerusalem a little before this time, how many of the apostles did he find in the city? See Gal. 1:18 and 19. Where were the others?
3. Locate Lydda on your outline map, and mark it with a cross, for there were "saints" at Lydda.
4. Æneas (Eneas) is a Greek name. Probably this Æneas was a Greek Jew.
5. Sharon, not indicated on the map, was a fertile plain lying between Joppa and Cæsarea along the sea.
6. Locate and mark Joppa on your map.
7. Verse 36: The woman named in this verse seems to have been a Greek-speaking Jewess. Her Greek name Dorcas (*gazelle*) is a translation of her Hebrew name Tabitha (*gazelle*).
8. The fact that Peter lodged in the house of a tanner (verse 43) is significant. The trade of tanning was an abomination to the Jews. Peter sets aside this prejudice to lodge with Simon. It was no great step to go next into the home of the Gentile Cornelius.

LESSON THOUGHT: Little did Peter know, when he went out on his preaching tour, that in the providence of God he would be the means of extending the Gospel to the Gentiles, and that this step would prepare the Church for the still greater labors of St. Paul.

STUDY VIII.—𝕮𝖍𝖊 𝕲𝖔𝖘𝖕𝖊𝖑 𝖎𝖘 𝕰𝖝𝖙𝖊𝖓𝖉𝖊𝖉 𝖙𝖔 𝖙𝖍𝖊 𝕲𝖊𝖓𝖙𝖎𝖑𝖊𝖘
SECOND DAY: PETER AND THE GENTILE CORNELIUS

There was in Cæsarea a devout Roman centurion named Cornelius, who was seeking the favor of God. By means of a vision Cornelius was instructed to send messengers to Joppa for Simon Peter, who should tell him what he ought to do. While the messengers of the centurion were on their way to Joppa, Peter was made ready for his visit to Cornelius by a special revelation that taught him to set aside his Jewish scruples.

1. The vision of Cornelius: Read Acts 10:1-8.
2. What is the character of the centurions mentioned in the New Testament? See Matt. 8:5; Luke 23:47; Acts 27:1-3.
3. Cornelius was probably a proselyte. He attended the synagogue services, but was not circumcised, nor had he adopted the peculiar ceremonial rules of the Jews.
4. Many Gentiles had become dissatisfied with their religion. Heathen worship was not only superstitious, but also at times, and in some places, grossly immoral. The comparatively pure worship of the Jews was attractive to many thoughtful Gentiles, who as proselytes (or "comers") attended the synagogues.
5. The vision of Peter: Read Acts 10:9-18.
6. The Jews felt that physical contact with the Gentiles resulted in moral contamination. To enter the house of a Gentile, to eat with him, or to have any social relations with him, rendered a Jew ceremonially unfit for worship. A special revelation, therefore, was necessary to enable Peter to set aside his Jewish prejudices and go to the home of the Roman centurion.

PRAYER: "Speak, Lord, for Thy servant heareth. Grant us ears to hear, eyes to see, wills to obey, hearts to love; then declare what Thou wilt, reveal what Thou wilt, command what Thou wilt, demand what Thou wilt." *Amen.*

Study VIII.—**The Gospel is Extended to the Gentiles**
Third Day: Peter and the Gentile Cornelius (Continued)

When the messengers of Cornelius came to Joppa, Peter readily consented to accompany them back to Cæsarea. As soon as he had arrived at Cæsarea, Cornelius made known to him his vision, and begged him to declare fully the will of God.

1. Read Acts 10:19-33.
2. What have you inferred concerning the personal influence of Cornelius? See verses 7 and 24.
3. Why was it an "unlawful thing" for a Jew to keep company with a man of another nation?
4. Do you think that Peter knew why he had been sent to visit Cornelius?
5. Has the Gospel been preached as yet to the Gentiles?

In view of the subject of to-day's lesson and that of to-morrow, consider briefly the standpoint of the Jewish Christian: The Jews were the chosen people of God; to them God had revealed Himself through prophets and holy men of old; to them Jesus, the Messiah, was sent. The Jews were bidden to keep themselves pure from Gentile defilements. Proud of the favor of God in the past, and proud of their superiority to the despised Gentiles, the Jewish Christians looked upon the Christian Church as the consummation of the Jewish Church. The first Christians were all Jews; what more natural than for them to think that a Gentile, to become a Christian, must first become a Jew, be circumcised, and keep all the Law of Moses? They were slow to see that the Gospel was for all, without the trammels of the Mosaic Law. Peter was taught this truth by a special revelation; yet the remaining apostles were reluctant to accept it, and a strong party soon formed of those who believed in Christianity for Jews only, or for Gentiles who had become Jews in all outward respects. This latter party bitterly opposed Paul in his work of extending the Church to the Gentiles.

Study VIII.—𝔗𝔥𝔢 𝔊𝔬𝔰𝔭𝔢𝔩 𝔦𝔰 𝔈𝔵𝔱𝔢𝔫𝔡𝔢𝔡 𝔱𝔬 𝔱𝔥𝔢 𝔊𝔢𝔫𝔱𝔦𝔩𝔢𝔰

FOURTH DAY: CORNELIUS AND HIS HOUSEHOLD ARE CONVERTED

As soon as Peter had heard the words of Cornelius, he uttered a momentous saying which clearly indicated that he for the first time saw the scope of the plan of salvation: "Of a truth I perceive that God is no respecter of persons, but in every nation he that feareth him, and worketh righteousness, is accepted with him." Peter then preached a brief sermon, after which the Holy Spirit descended with power upon all present.

1. Read Acts 10:34-48.
2. Why was it important that the recognition of the right of the Gentiles to salvation should come first from Peter?
3. Verses 44-46: The Pentecost of Acts, chapter 2, was a Jewish Pentecost. This is a Gentile Pentecost, accompanied, like its great predecessor, with a gift of tongues.
4. In the Old Testament the promise was made that Salvation should come to the Gentiles:
    (a) At the time of the call of Abraham: Genesis 12:3.
    (b) In the time of Isaiah: Isaiah 52:10.
    (c) By the prophet Zephaniah: Zeph. 2:11.
   In the New Testament similar promises are found:
    (d) In the words of Simeon: Luke 2:32.
    (e) The words of Jesus: John 10:16.
5. How do you suppose Peter spent the time while he tarried in the house of Cornelius?

PRAYER: "O Lord, grant all who contend for the faith, never to injure it by clamor and impatience; but, speaking Thy precious truth in love, so to present it that it may be loved, and that men may see in it Thy goodness and beauty." *Amen.*

STUDY VIII.—**The Gospel is Extended to the Gentiles**
FIFTH DAY: PETER CRITICISED FOR HAVING EATEN WITH GENTILES

Before Peter returned from Cæsarea, it became known in Jerusalem that he had not only been associating with Gentiles, but had actually eaten with them. On his arrival at Jerusalem those Jewish Christians who were most zealous for the ceremonial law criticised him for his conduct; to justify himself, therefore, Peter rehearsed the whole story from the beginning.

1. Read Acts 11:1-18.
2. Verse 2: "They of the circumcision." Already the Jewish Christians had begun to divide into a conservative and a liberal party. The conservative party—they of the circumcision—while adopting Christianity, still clung tenaciously to the ritual and ceremonial laws of Judaism. The liberal party, consisting chiefly of Greek Jews, were less tenacious of those laws, and were more ready to recognize the claims of the Gentiles.
3. Verse 18: The conservative party was silenced for a time, but before long they were at work again, trying to prevent the free extension of the Gospel to the Gentiles. They held that all Gentiles, in order to embrace Christianity, must first become Jews. This party bitterly opposed the Apostle Paul, and tried repeatedly to kill him, as will be learned in later lessons.

THOUGHT FOR THE DAY: Do you ever think what a virtue it is to be free from prejudice in religious matters? Men differ honestly and conscientiously regarding religious rites, ceremonies, and doctrines. Do you have charity enough to regard those men who do not belong to your own church or creed as your Christian brethren?

Study VIII.—**The Gospel is Extended to the Gentiles**

Sixth Day: The Gospel Is Preached to Greeks at Antioch

Through the preaching of Peter the conversion of the Roman centurion took place and prepared the apostles at Jerusalem for the extension of the Gospel to the Gentiles. Meanwhile, those Christians who were scattered abroad by persecution "went everywhere preaching the word." Among these men were some Greek Jews who in Antioch preached to Greeks and brought about their conversion. On learning of this, the apostles sent Barnabas to Antioch. Barnabas was greatly pleased with the work of the Greek Jews, and realizing that Paul was the man above all others fitted by birth and training for such a field, brought him from Tarsus to Antioch.

1. Read Acts 11:19-26.
2. Mark with a cross on your outline map Phœnicia (Phenice), Cyprus, and Antioch.
3. Verse 20: In this verse the R.V. gives "Greeks," which is supported by the best MSS. The A.V. has "Grecians," i. e., "Greek Jews," which does not make good sense when compared with the latter part of verse 19.
4. Antioch was one of the most important cities of the Roman Empire. According to Josephus, only Rome and Alexandria took precedence of it.
5. Paul probably came to Antioch in 44 A.D.
6. Verse 25: Why did Barnabas think of Paul at this time and choose him for this work?
7. Before the name "Christian" was used, what names were given to the members of the new Church? See Acts 5:14; 9:26; 9:32.

Each of the three world-nations contributed to the name "Christian": From the language of the Jews came the word *Messiah*, which means "Anointed"; the Greek word used to translate this is Χριστός (*Christos*), *Christ*, the "Anointed One"; to this was added an ending *-ianos* after the Roman fashion; for the Romans often formed party names by adding *-ianus* to the names of leaders; as, *Pompeiani*, "followers of Pompey," *Cæsariani*, "followers of Cæsar," etc. The *Christiani,* or "Christians," are therefore the "followers of Christ."

STUDY VIII.—𝔗𝔥𝔢 𝔊𝔬𝔰𝔭𝔢𝔩 𝔦𝔰 𝔈𝔵𝔱𝔢𝔫𝔡𝔢𝔡 𝔱𝔬 𝔱𝔥𝔢 𝔊𝔢𝔫𝔱𝔦𝔩𝔢𝔰

SEVENTH DAY: BARNABAS AND PAUL VISIT JERUSALEM

While Barnabas and Paul were working earnestly among the Gentiles at Antioch, a famine broke out in Judea. With true Christian generosity and charity the Church at Antioch determined to send relief to their brethren at Jerusalem. Paul and Barnabas were dispatched upon this errand, and after no great time returned to Antioch.

1. Read Acts 11:27-30.
2. This famine is supposed to have taken place in 45 A.D.
3. Read Acts 12:25.
4. The first twenty-four verses of chapter 12 are not included in these studies. Verses 1 and 2 contain the statement that James, the brother of John, was put to death by Herod. It is narrated also that Peter, imprisoned by Herod, made his escape by Divine help (verses 3-19). The remainder of the chapter is taken up with an account of the death of Herod (44 A.D.). It must not be thought because the account of the death of Herod intervenes between the account of the journey of Paul and Barnabas to Jerusalem and the account of their return to Antioch, that they were necessarily in Jerusalem in 44 A.D.
5. How was John Mark related to Barnabas? See Col. 4:10.

PRAYER: "O God, who hast ordained that whatever is to be desired, should be sought by labor, and who, by Thy blessing, bringest honest labor to good effect; look with mercy on my studies and endeavors. Grant me calmness of mind and steadiness of purpose, that I may so do Thy will in this short life, as to obtain happiness in the world to come, for the sake of Jesus Christ our Lord." *Amen.*

PART IV

Paul's First Missionary Journey

Study IX.—Missions in Cyprus, Perga, and Pisidian Antioch
Study X.—Missions in Iconium, Derbe, and Lystra: The Return to Antioch in Syria
Study XI.—A Crisis: Must Gentile Christians Keep the Mosaic Law?

STUDY IX.—**Missions in Cyprus, Perga, and Pisidian Antioch**

FIRST DAY: BARNABAS AND PAUL CHOSEN FOR MISSIONARY WORK: THEY GO TO CYPRUS

Antioch was the first city in which Gentiles were converted in any considerable numbers; it was a city also in which Jewish conservatism and exclusiveness were far less marked than in Jerusalem. Hence Antioch, rather than Jerusalem, became the headquarters for missionary work among the Gentiles.

Leaving Antioch, Barnabas and Paul went first to the island of Cyprus.

1. Read Acts 13:1-3.
2. Verse 2: Did Paul know before this time that he was to preach among the Gentiles?
3. It took great courage and faith on the part of Barnabas and Paul to go on this mission to Gentile lands. As Jews they would be obliged to meet the contempt which Gentiles felt toward Jews; as Christians they would be obliged to incur the hatred which the unbelieving Jews extended to all who adopted the new religion.
4. How was Paul specially fitted for his work as a missionary in view of the following qualifications:
   (a) His training as a Rabbi?
   (b) His knowledge of Hebrew, Aramaic, and Greek?
   (c) His Roman citizenship?
   (d) His trade?
5. Read Acts 13:4 and 5.
6. Locate Seleucia, Cyprus, and Salamis.
7. Had the Gospel been preached in Cyprus before this time? See Acts 11:19.
8. Mark Salamis with a cross on your outline map.
9. What relationship existed between Barnabas and John? Read first, Acts 12:25, then Colossians 4:10.

THOUGHT FOR THE DAY: As the disciples earnestly sought God's will, the Holy Ghost directed them to take up a special work (verse 2). If you will sincerely and honestly seek to help the spread of God's Kingdom, and will put yourself in His hands to be used as He sees fit, you will be startled and amazed at the many opportunities you will have for service.

Study IX.—**Missions in Cyprus, Perga, and Pisidian Antioch**

SECOND DAY: PAUL AND BARNABAS AT PAPHOS: PAUL AND ELYMAS THE SORCERER

Leaving Salamis, Barnabas and Paul journeyed through Cyprus until they reached Paphos, on the western coast. Here a sorcerer named Elymas sought, from selfish reasons, to oppose the work of the apostles. At the command of Paul, Elymas was smitten with blindness.

1. Read Acts 13:6-12.
2. Paphos was the seat of the worship of Aphrodite; it was also the residence of the Roman proconsul of Cyprus.
3. Why did the proconsul (or "deputy," as he is called in the A.V.), if he was "a man of understanding," have with him the sorcerer and false prophet Bar-jesus? Does the latter part of verse 7 throw any light on this point?
4. What motive had Elymas in opposing Barnabas and Saul?
5. Verse 9: Beginning with this verse, Luke uses the name *Paul* instead of *Saul* throughout the remainder of Acts. What reason can you assign for this change?
6. This is the first passage in which Paul speaks at length; he now comes to the front as a leader, and takes the initiative against Elymas; his rapidity of action is characteristic. Henceforth he occupies the first place in the narrative, while Barnabas is secondary.
7. Mark Paphos on your map with a cross.

PRAYER: "O Lord, give us grace never to parley with temptation, never to tamper with conscience; never to spare the right eye, or hand, or foot that is a snare to us; never to lose our souls, though in exchange we should gain the whole world." *Amen.*

STUDY IX.—**Missions in Cyprus, Perga, and Pisidian Antioch**

THIRD DAY: PAUL GOES FROM CYPRUS TO ANTIOCH IN PISIDIA

On leaving Cyprus, Paul and his company sailed to the southern coast of Asia Minor. When they reached Perga in Pamphylia, John Mark left them. Paul and Barnabas then proceeded through Pamphylia to Antioch of Pisidia, where Paul, as was his custom, went into the synagogue of the Jews upon the Sabbath day.

1. Read Acts 13:13-15.
2. Notice in verse 13 that Paul is now recognized as leader. Before this time Luke has always spoken of them as "Barnabas and Saul." Henceforth it is "Paul and Barnabas."
3. Perga was an unimportant city of Pamphylia, about eight miles from the sea. Locate Perga upon the map.
4. At Perga, John Mark left the apostles and returned home. His reasons for leaving are not known. He may have been displeased because Paul had supplanted Barnabas as leader; he may have feared the dangers lying before them in Pamphylia and Pisidia—the turbulent streams, rugged mountains, rough roads, fierce brigands, and wild, rude peoples speaking strange dialects.
5. Antioch was an important city for missionary work; it was the center of a *regio,* or subdivision, of the province of Galatia.
6. Paul enters the synagogue on the Sabbath day and takes part in the worship. The main features of the worship of the synagogue are the following:
   (a) Prayers and opening ritual.
   (b) Reading from the Scriptures:
      1. The "First Lesson," from the *Law* (Genesis, Exodus, Leviticus, Numbers, and Deuteronomy).
      2. The "Second Lesson," from the *Prophets* (Joshua, Judges, Ruth, 1 and 2 Samuel, 1 and 2 Kings, Isaiah, Jeremiah, Ezekiel, and the twelve minor prophets).
   (c) An address or sermon.

There was no regular preacher. After the reading of the Scriptures, learned men or strangers who chanced to be present would, at the request of the officers of the synagogue, address the congregation. Read Luke 4:14-21.

Study IX.—**Missions in Cyprus, Perga, and Pisidian Antioch**

Fourth Day: Paul's Sermon at Antioch in Pisidia

At the request of the synagogue officers, Paul delivered an address or sermon in the synagogue of Antioch to a congregation composed of Jews and Gentiles. To-day's lesson is a study of the first two parts of Paul's sermon.

1. Read Acts 13:16-25.
2. It should be remembered that in this, as in all the speeches and addresses of the book of Acts, Luke gives only an epitome of the words of the speakers.
3. Verse 16: "Beckoning with the hand." Paul's gestures are several times alluded to: See Acts 21:40; 26:1.
4. In what language did Paul deliver this address?
5. In verse 16, who are those whom Paul designates as "ye that fear God"?
6. Verses 16-25 contain a skilful abridgment of Jewish history from the call of Abraham to the ministry of John the Baptist. What sermons have you studied already that begin in the same way?
7. Paul's sermon consists of four parts:
   I. A Historical Introduction—From Abraham to David.
   II. The Messiah is Jesus.
   III. The Death and Resurrection of Jesus.
   IV. Salvation by faith in Jesus Christ.
8. The verses in to-day's lesson constitute the first two parts of Paul's sermon. Write the four heads of his sermon in your notebook and designate the verses that belong to each part.
9. Mark Antioch (in Pisidia) with a cross on your outline map.

Thought for To-day: The whole Old Testament looks forward to Jesus Christ; the whole New Testament looks back upon Him. Yet the writers of the Old and New Testament do not spend their thought and effort alone in mere contemplation of His character and in mere worship of His glory; they both alike agree in proclaiming that His salvation is for all men in every land.

Study IX.—**Missions in Cyprus, Perga, and Pisidian Antioch**

Fifth Day: Paul's Sermon at Antioch in Pisidia (Continued)

To-day's lesson is the study of the third part of Paul's sermon in the synagogue of Pisidian Antioch. The topic is "The Death and Resurrection of Jesus."

1. Read Acts 13:26-37.
2. As may be learned from verse 26, what two classes of people were in the synagogue congregation?
3. Verse 27: At what point in the synagogue services were the "prophets" read? See page 69, section 6.
4. Verse 31: For how many days after His resurrection was Christ seen? Acts 1:3.
5. Verse 33: What verse of the second Psalm is here quoted?
6. Verse 35: The quotation is taken from the sixteenth Psalm. Which verse?
7. At the very center of the teaching of the apostles is the doctrine of the resurrection of Christ. Paul was converted six years after the resurrection of Christ; he could, therefore, hear from the lips of eyewitnesses the story of Christ's liberation from the tomb; he was a well-trained, keen-witted Rabbi. It is not likely that any fabricated or false account would have imposed upon Paul.

St. Paul on the Resurrection: "Now if Christ be preached that he rose from the dead, how say some among you that there is no resurrection of the dead? But if there be no resurrection of the dead, then Christ is not risen: and if Christ be not risen, then is our preaching vain, and your faith is also vain. Yea, and we are found false witnesses of God; because we have testified of God that he raised up Christ; whom he raised not up, if so be that the dead rise not."—*First Epistle to the Corinthians* 15:12-15.

Study IX.—Missions in Cyprus, Perga, and Pisidian Antioch

Sixth Day: Paul's Sermon at Antioch in Pisidia (Continued)

Paul sums up his argument with the statement that men are justified or brought into right relations with God, not by doing the works of the Jewish Law, but by faith in Jesus Christ. In closing, the apostle solemnly warns his hearers not to despise this offer of divine grace.

1. Read Acts 13:38-43.
2. Verse 39: This verse contains the germ of Paul's later preaching and teaching: Man had sought righteousness by obeying the precepts of the Mosaic Law; but he could not, by mere conformity to rules and laws, measure up to the standard required of him—he was too imperfect, too much inclined toward sin. Belief in Christ, and acceptance of His righteousness, would alone justify man—that is, make him righteous in the sight of God.
3. Verse 41: The quotation is from Habakkuk, chapter 1. Locate the verse.
4. Verse 42: Certain words of this verse, as given in the A.V., are not found in the best Greek manuscripts. In the R.V. the verse runs: "And as they went out, they besought that these words might be spoken to them the next Sabbath."
5. Verse 43: The "religious proselytes" were probably native Pisidians.

Faith and the Law: "We who are Jews by nature, and not sinners of the Gentiles, knowing that a man is not justified by the works of the law, but by the faith of Jesus Christ, even we have believed in Jesus Christ, that we might be justified by the faith of Christ, and not by the works of the law: for by the works of the law shall no flesh be justified."—St. Paul, *Epistle to the Galatians* 2:15 and 16.

STUDY IX.—**Missions in Cyprus, Perga, and Pisidian Antioch**

SEVENTH DAY: THE SPREAD OF THE GOSPEL IN PISIDIA

On the Sabbath following Paul's sermon in the synagogue at Antioch, a vast congregation of Gentiles gathered to hear the apostles. The Jews, since they had been unable to attract such multitudes to the synagogue, were filled with envy; they opposed the work of the apostles and sought, by blasphemous words, to overthrow their teaching. Thereupon the apostles turned to the Gentiles, and worked among them with such success that the whole region heard the Gospel.

1. Read Acts 13:44-49.
2. What statements of the apostles did the Jews contradict (verse 45)?
3. Verse 46: Why was it necessary that the Word of God should be preached to the Jews first?
4. Verse 47: Locate this quotation, which may be found in Isaiah, chapter 49.
5. Verse 48: The phrase, "As many as were ordained to eternal life," seems to mean, "as many as had disposed themselves toward eternal life."
6. It does not seem that the stay of Paul and Barnabas in Antioch was long, yet such was their activity and such the spirit of their converts, that the whole region speedily heard the Gospel.
7. Note the use of the word *region* in verse 49. It has a specific meaning here, and refers to that portion of the province of Galatia in which Antioch lay. In Acts 14:6 the Lycaonian *region* of Galatia is mentioned.
8. Review questions: Since leaving Antioch on this missionary journey what cities has Paul visited? What important incidents have taken place in connection with his work in these cities?

Study X.—**Missions in Iconium, Derbe, and Lystra: The Return to Antioch in Syria**

First Day: Paul and Barnabas Flee to Iconium

So successful were Paul and Barnabas in their labors at Antioch that the unbelieving Jews were filled with envy and rage, and immediately undertook a vigorous persecution of the apostles. To escape this, Paul and Barnabas left Antioch and fled to Iconium, a city on the borders of Lycaonia.

1. Read Acts 13:50-52.
2. Verse 50: "The devout women of honorable estate" (R.V.) were Gentile proselytes; they were women of rank, the wives of the chief men of the city. The "chief men of the city" were probably the Roman authorities. How is it that the Jews were able to get the help of these men and women against the apostles?
3. In the verses of to-day's lesson the apostles obey three commands of Christ:
   (a) To flee from persecution: Matt. 10:23.
   (b) To shake off the dust of the feet in condemnation: Matt. 10:14.
   (c) To rejoice in persecution: Matt. 5:11 and 12.

Memory Passage: "We glory in tribulations also: knowing that tribulation worketh patience; and patience, experience; and experience, hope; and hope maketh not ashamed; because the love of God is shed abroad in our hearts by the Holy Ghost which is given unto us."—St. Paul, *Epistle to the Romans* 5:3-5.

Prayer: "Help us to realize, dear Lord, that our trials and troubles may be a means unto us for gaining strength of character; let us never be discouraged, but enable us to trust in Thee. Let our light affliction, which is but for a moment, work for us a far more exceeding and eternal weight of glory." *Amen.*

STUDY X.—**Missions in Iconium, Derbe, and Lystra: The Return to Antioch in Syria**

SECOND DAY: THE GOSPEL IN ICONIUM: THE APOSTLES FLEE INTO LYCAONIA.

After their arrival at Iconium, Paul and Barnabas spoke with such effect in the synagogue of the city that a multitude of Jews and Greeks believed; but, just as at Antioch, the unbelieving Jews stirred up the Gentiles against the apostles. Paul and Barnabas then fled to Lystra and Derbe, cities of Lycaonia.

1. Read Acts 14:1-7.
2. Locate Iconium, and mark it with a cross upon your outline map.
3. Iconium was an important city on the borders of Lycaonia, near the great trade route stretching from Ephesus to the Euphrates. The situation of Iconium made it an especially desirable center for missionary work.
4. Verse 2: The unbelieving Jews stirred up such of the Gentiles as were favorably disposed to the worship of the synagogue, but who had not adopted the teachings of the apostles.
5. Verse 4: The multitude of the city was divided into a Christian body and a non-Christian body. Of what saying of Christ's is this the fulfilment? See Luke 12:51-53.
6. Locate Lystra and Derbe, and mark them with crosses on your outline map.

PRAYER: "O Lord, give us more charity, more self-denial, more likeness to Thee. Teach us to sacrifice our comforts to others, and our likings for the sake of doing good. Make us kindly in thought, gentle in word, generous in deed. Teach us that it is better to give than to receive; better to forget ourselves than to put ourselves forward; better to minister than to be ministered unto. And unto Thee, the God of Love, be glory and praise for ever." *Amen.*

STUDY X.—**Missions in Iconium, Derbe, and Lystra: The Return to Antioch in Syria**

THIRD DAY: PAUL AND BARNABAS REGARDED AS GODS BY THE LYCAONIANS

At Lystra, Paul healed a cripple who had been lame from birth. This miracle so astonished the Lycaonians that they thought Paul and Barnabas were gods in the guise of men.

1. Read Acts 14:8-13.
2. Observe how minute and accurate are the words of Luke in describing the infirmity of the cripple. What was Luke's profession?
3. Why did Paul think that the cripple had faith to be healed?
4. Verse 11: The Lycaonians were apparently bi-lingual: they spoke both their native Lycaonian dialect and Greek. In their astonishment at Paul's miracle they lapse into their native tongue.

In this region was laid the scene of the story of Philemon and Baucis, narrated by Ovid: Once on a time Jupiter and Mercury came down to earth disguised as travelers. They sought entertainment at several doors, but were turned away. Finally, in a humble cottage, an aged pair, Philemon and Baucis, from their scanty store set forth food before the wayfarers. At the conclusion of the meal the gods revealed themselves to the pious couple, and granted them long life as guardians of a holy temple. Perhaps the men of Lycaonia had this story in mind at this time.

"In ancient art Jupiter was always represented as a tall, majestic and benignant figure, while Mercury was the small, swift messenger of the father of gods and men." From verse 12, therefore, what do you infer concerning the personal appearance of Barnabas and Paul?

Study X.—**Missions in Iconium, Derbe, and Lystra: The Return to Antioch in Syria**

Fourth Day: Paul and Barnabas Regarded as Gods by the Lycaonians (Continued)

When the apostles heard that the men of Lystra were about to offer sacrifice to them as gods, they rushed among them, and restrained them from carrying out their intention.

1. Read Acts 14:14-18.
2. Verses 15-17: These verses, in all probability, contain only a few of the things said by Paul and Barnabas at this time.
3. In certain of these early addresses of Paul may be found the germs of many ideas which he afterward expanded more fully. With verse 16 compare Acts 17:30, a verse in a speech delivered by Paul at Athens.
4. Verse 17: "He left not himself without witness"; that is, among the non-Jewish nations. To them He had spoken through the wonders of nature, sending them the fruits of the earth in their season. The thought of verse 17 Paul expands in his *Epistle to the Romans*. Read Romans 1:18-21.
5. After the event narrated in the lessons of yesterday and to-day, Paul and Barnabas seem to have labored successfully in Lystra. Among the converts of Paul was the youthful Timothy, who afterward became his faithful companion and helper. That he was a convert of Paul's preaching seems clear from 1 Timothy 1:2; that he was converted at this particular time seems likely from the fact that he is spoken of as being already a disciple at the time of Paul's second visit to Lystra: Acts 16:1. For Timothy's parentage, see Acts 16:1.

Thought for To-day: With verse 17 of to-day's lesson compare Romans 2:4. Do these verses apply at all to you?

Study X.—**Missions in Iconium, Derbe, and Lystra: The Return to Antioch in Syria**

Fifth Day: The Apostles Driven from Lystra: They Return to Pisidian Antioch

For some time there was no opposition to the work of the apostles at Lystra. After a while, however, certain Jews came down from Antioch and Iconium, and stirred up a persecution against Paul and Barnabas. Paul was stoned. The apostles then left Lystra, and went to Derbe. Later they returned through Lystra and Iconium to Antioch in Pisidia.

1. Read Acts 14:19-23.
2. Verses 19 and 20:
    (a) The Lycaonians in ancient times bore the reputation of being fickle: Aristotle says they were "faithless." Hence they were easily induced to turn against the apostles.
    (b) Paul alludes to this stoning in one of his Epistles: See 2 Cor. 11:25.
    (c) Picture to yourself the scene: Paul bleeding and unconscious upon the ground, with the disciples standing sorrowfully about him.
    (d) Perhaps Paul stayed overnight in the house of Timothy's parents. Do you suppose that Paul recalled at this time the stoning of Stephen?
3. Verse 21: The apostles seem to have spent some little time at Derbe. The return journey was probably made rapidly, perhaps even secretly, for fear of the Jews.
4. Verse 23: For a similar action, see Acts 13:3. For what purpose were elders ordained in every city?

Prayer: "O holy and ever blessed Lord, teach us, we beseech Thee, to love one another, to exercise forbearance and forgiveness toward our enemies; to recompense no man evil for evil, but to be merciful even as Thou, our Father in Heaven, art merciful; that so we may continually follow after Thee in all our doings, and be more and more conformed to Thine image and likeness." *Amen.*

Study X.—**Missions in Iconium, Derbe, and Lystra: The Return to Antioch in Syria**

Sixth Day: From Pisidian Antioch to Antioch in Syria

The apostles returned from Antioch in Pisidia to Perga in Pamphylia, then went overland to Attalia, whence they sailed for Antioch in Syria. On their arrival at home they gathered together the Church, and told them all that God had wrought through them.

1. Read Acts 14:24-28.
2. Did the apostles preach at Perga when in the city on their way inland? Mark Perga with a cross.
3. When Paul and Barnabas came to Perga the first time they came from Cyprus on a vessel which ascended the Cestrus River as far as Perga. Now on the return journey they apparently fail to find at Perga a vessel bound for Syria, and so go overland to Attalia, 16 miles distant, where they embark for Syria.
4. The towns of Antioch in Pisidia, Iconium, Lystra, and Derbe were all included in the Roman province of Galatia. To the churches of these towns Paul later addressed his *Epistle to the Galatians*. Certain peculiarities of the Galatians, and certain features of Paul's visit among them, should be noted at this time.
    (a) The Galatians heard the Gospel readily, but were soon turned away by false teachers. See Galatians 1:6.
    (b) This fickleness of the Galatian character has already been noticed in the case of the Lycaonians. See page 78, section 2 (a).
    (c) Paul was ill while in Galatia: Galatians 4:13 and 14.
5. "God . . . had opened the door of faith unto the Gentiles" (verse 27, end). Perhaps Paul himself was the one who made use of the figure of speech, and Luke may be quoting him. Paul uses a similar expression in one of his letters: 1 Corinthians 16:9.

Memory Passage: Memorize the saying of Jesus found in John 10:9.

STUDY X.—**Missions in Iconium, Derbe, and Lystra: The Return to Antioch in Syria**

SEVENTH DAY: REVIEW LESSON

As stated in the lesson of yesterday, when the apostles had returned to Antioch in Syria, they called together the Church, and told the story of their successful missionary tour in Cyprus and Asia Minor.

1. Without referring to your Bible or to these *Studies,* write in your note-book a list of the places visited by Paul on this first missionary journey.
2. What were the chief events in each town or city?
3. What important doctrine does Paul state for the first time—a doctrine that became the very center of his preaching?
4. What difficulties had Paul met in his efforts to spread the Gospel among the Gentiles?
5. In the closing years of his life Paul still remembered this journey as one of great hardship. Read 2 Timothy 3:11.
6. Some conclusions that Paul may have reached after his return from this first missionary tour:
    (a) The Jews were not unwilling to listen to the Gospel; but when it was proposed that the Gentiles should join the Christian Church without first becoming Jews, they rebelled.
    (b) The Gentiles were ready for the Gospel, and received it gladly.
    (c) The question of the relation of the Gentiles to the Mosaic Law was one that would have to be settled in the near future.
    (d) Paul must have begun to see that the Law had served its purpose in training the Jews, and was now a useless thing.

PAUL ON THE WORK OF THE LAW: "Before faith came, we were kept under the law, shut up unto the faith which should afterward be revealed. Wherefore the law was our schoolmaster, to bring us to Christ, that we might be justified by faith. But after that faith is come we are no longer under a schoolmaster. For ye are all children of God by faith in Christ Jesus. . . . There is neither Jew nor Greek, there is neither bond nor free, there is neither male nor female: for ye are all one in Christ Jesus."—*Epistle to the Galatians* 3:23-28.

Study XI.—A Crisis: Must Gentile Christians Keep the Mosaic Law?

First Day: Paul Goes to Jerusalem to Ask Freedom for the Gentiles.

Thus far the opposition which Paul had met in the spread of the Gospel came from the unbelieving Jews and from Gentiles who had been stirred up by the Jews. Trouble now arose within the Church itself: certain Christian Jews came down from Jerusalem to Antioch and began to teach that the Gentiles in the Church must be circumcised and keep the Mosaic Law. Paul and Barnabas, with others, went to Jerusalem to discuss this question with the leaders of the Church.

1. Read Acts 15:1-5.
2. Verse 1: The men from Judea were not officially sent, nor were they authorized to handle this matter. See Acts 15:24.
3. The Jews felt that they were contaminated by contact with the Gentiles. The Gentiles did not purify themselves according to the ceremonial law; they ate the flesh of swine and other food unclean from the Jewish point of view. Consequently the Jews were averse to sharing with them the Lord's Supper and associating with them socially. The one sign and test of a Jew was circumcision. This the Jewish extremists determined to force on Gentile Christians.
4. Verse 3: Had the Gospel been preached before this time in Phœnicia? See Acts 11:19.
5. Verse 4: On what points do you suppose that Paul and Barnabas would lay the most emphasis in this review of their work?
6. What were the beliefs and practices of the sect of the Pharisees?

Paul the Champion of the Gentiles: Throughout his life Paul fought for the freedom of the Gentiles from the claims of the Jewish Law. His writings abound in powerful arguments on this matter. And to Paul, more than anyone else, is due the fact that the Christian Church did not become a sect of Judaism. Paul settled the question forever: a few years after his death it ceased to be an issue.

Study XI.—A Crisis: Must Gentile Christians Keep the Mosaic Law?

Second Day: The Council at Jerusalem: Peter's Speech

After some little time had been spent in private conference and informal discussion, the men from Antioch gathered together with the apostles and elders of the Jerusalem Church to debate the question that had arisen. After considerable discussion of a noisy character, Peter spoke in favor of freedom for the Gentile Christians, and Barnabas and Paul told of the wonders God had wrought through them among the Gentiles.

1. Read Acts 15:6-12.
2. Verse 7:
    (a) To what event does Peter refer in this verse?
    (b) How long before this had the event taken place?
3. Verses 8 and 9: Has Peter used this argument at all before in the book of Acts? If so, where?
4. Verse 10: What does Peter mean by the word "yoke"? Does he refer to the actual laws of Moses—the written law, or to the laws compiled and added by the scribes and Pharisees—the oral law?
5. What did Jesus say about the oppression of the Law? See Matt. 23:2-4.
6. The cases of conversion among the Gentiles which Paul and Barnabas gave were concrete examples of the principle laid down by Peter in verses 8 and 9.

Salvation the Gift of God: The keynote of Peter's speech is *salvation by the grace (or favor) of God*. St. Paul's statement of this principle is in Ephesians 2:4-8: "God, who is rich in mercy, for his great love wherewith he loved us, even when we were dead in sins, hath quickened us together with Christ (by grace are ye saved) and hath raised us up together, and made us sit together in heavenly places in Christ Jesus: that in the ages to come he might show the exceeding riches of his grace in his kindness toward us through Christ Jesus. For by grace are ye saved through faith."

Study XI.—A Crisis: Must Gentile Christians Keep the Mosaic Law?

Third Day: The Council (Continued): The Speech of James

The course of the debate thus far may be summarized as follows: The Judaizing party had vehemently argued that the Gentiles should be circumcised and keep the Law; Peter spoke next in behalf of the Gentiles, narrating how God through him had bestowed the Holy Spirit on the Gentile Cornelius and his family; last of all, Paul and Barnabas told in detail the story of the conversion of the Gentiles in Asia Minor.

Both sides of the question had now been presented. Thereupon James, the brother of Jesus, arose and proposed a fair and just compromise.

1. Read Acts 15:13-21.
2. Verse 13: James was the brother of Jesus and author of the Epistle that bears his name. "A sense of awe clung about him and all he said and did. Clothed with a mysterious and indefinable dignity as 'the brother of the Lord,' that dignity and mystery were enhanced by his bearing, dress, manner of life, and entire appearance. Tradition represents him as wearing no wool, but clothed in fine white linen from head to foot. It is said that he was so holy, and so highly esteemed by the whole Jewish people, that he alone was allowed, like the High Priest, to enter the Holy Place; that he lived a celibate and ascetic life; and that he spent long hours alone in the temple praying for the people."—*Canon Farrar.*
3. James represents the conservative side of the council. After citing certain prophecies regarding the coming of the Gentiles to the Lord, he proposes a fair compromise.
4. Upon certain commandments given to Noah, the Rabbis had built up the seven so-called "Noachian Laws." The four prohibitions of James in verse 20 embody three or possibly four of these laws.
5. If Jews and Gentiles were to work and live harmoniously in the same Church it was necessary that they should grant one another certain concessions, and respect one another's feelings.

Thought for the Day: What did Jesus say of those who, like James, were peacemakers? Matt. 5:9.

Study XI.—**A Crisis: Must Gentile Christians Keep the Mosaic Law?**

FOURTH DAY: THE DECISION OF THE COUNCIL

The proposal made by James, that the Gentiles be asked to observe only four prohibitions underlying the Mosaic Law, was adopted. These prohibitions were embodied in a letter drawn up by the council and sent to the Gentiles of Antioch, Syria, and Cilicia.

1. Read Acts 15:22-29.
2. Judas, surnamed Barsabas, of verse 22, is otherwise unknown. Silas, of the same verse, is the one who later was the companion of Paul upon his second missionary journey.
3. It is evident that the letter was written in Greek:
    (a) The persons addressed were Gentiles.
    (b) The letter has the form usually followed by Greek writers: at the beginning the name of the writer; then that of the person addressed, followed by the body of the letter proper; at the end a farewell salutation.
4. This letter is one of the earliest epistles of the apostolic period.
5. Verse 23: When and by whom was the Cilician church founded?
6. The men who had begun the trouble at Antioch were unauthorized persons from Jerusalem. Judas and Silas, who now visit Antioch, are fully empowered to state the views of the Jerusalem Church.
7. Verse 25: Observe the kind and affectionate manner in which Barnabas and Paul are here mentioned. Why does the name of Barnabas precede that of Paul?

THOUGHT FOR THE DAY: Especially noteworthy is the calm and conciliatory tone of the letter sent by the Jerusalem churches to the Gentiles of Antioch, Syria, and Cilicia. Memorize *Proverbs* 15:1.

Study XI.—A Crisis: Must Gentile Christians Keep the Mosaic Law?

Fifth Day: Paul's Own Account of the Council

In his *Epistle to the Galatians* Paul himself gives an account of the council at Jerusalem. This account is peculiar in some respects. Certain Jewish teachers, enemies of Paul, had tampered with his Galatian converts. By representing that Paul was not truly an apostle because he had not seen and heard Jesus, they endeavored to undermine his authority. Paul indignantly answers their charges in his letter to the Galatians; he says that he is an apostle "not of man, neither by man, but by Jesus Christ and God the Father" (Gal. 1:1). He gives a brief account of his life, and in narrating the events of the Jerusalem council emphasizes the fact that he was independent of the other apostles. Consequently, since he is laying stress upon certain features only of the conference, his own account is somewhat different from that of Luke in the book of Acts.

1. Read Galatians 2:1-10.
2. Verse 1: The "fourteen years" are fourteen years dating from the visit of Gal. 1:18. It was probably a little more than twelve years. See page 54, section 3.
3. Verse 2: By comparing the first clause of this verse with Acts 15:2, it seems that not only was Paul chosen by the Church at Antioch to go to Jerusalem, but also he was advised in a vision to go thither.
4. The private conference with the leaders mentioned in verse 2 probably took place before the public council was held. By this means James, Peter, and John—the "pillars" of the Church—were won over (verse 9).
5. Verse 10: This collection for the poor is not mentioned by Luke in Acts. Paul later gave much attention to the gathering of money for the poor at Jerusalem.

Lesson Thought: What phase of Paul's character do you discover in the lesson of to-day (Gal. 2:1-10)?

Study XI.—**A Crisis: Must Gentile Christians Keep the Mosaic Law?**

Sixth Day: Paul Returns from Jerusalem to Antioch: The Reading of an Apostolic Letter

Paul and Barnabas, with the messengers sent by the Jerusalem Church, returned to Antioch. As soon as they arrived, they called together the believers and read to them the letter from Jerusalem.

1. Read Acts 15:30-35.
2. How many persons can you name among those composing the company that went from Jerusalem to Antioch? See Acts 15:22 and 32, also Galatians 2:1.
3. Verse 31: The scene, when this apostolic letter was read, is the forerunner of the scenes later when letters from Paul were read in the churches to which he had written. A letter addressed to an individual church was often passed to other churches and read in them. See Colossians 4:16.
4. Verse 31: Both Jews and Gentiles would hear the letter read. What grounds had each party for "rejoicing for the consolation"?

Paul returned from Jerusalem more than ever conscious of his power and clear in his purposes. "Paul had made himself master of the situation. He had come to the very forefront in the guidance of the Church. The future of Christianity rested with the Gentiles, and to the Gentiles the acts and writings of Paul were to be of greater importance than those of all the other apostles. His Apostolate had been decisively recognized. He had met Peter and John and even the awe-inspiring brother of the Lord in conference, and found himself so completely their equal in the gifts of the Holy Ghost, that it was impossible for them to resist his credentials. . . . He had returned from Jerusalem more than ever conscious of himself, conscious of his own power, clear in his future purposes. He inspired into the Church at Antioch his own convictions with a force that no one could resist."—*Canon Farrar.*

Study XI.—A Crisis: Must Gentile Christians Keep the Mosaic Law?

Seventh Day: Peter's Visit to Antioch

Not long after the council at Jerusalem, Peter visited Antioch. While there he associated freely with Gentiles, and even ate with them. When, however, certain Jews came down from Jerusalem, Peter withdrew himself from the Gentiles. In like manner also some of the Antiochian Jews then separated themselves from the Gentiles, and even Barnabas was led to change his attitude toward the Gentile converts. This inconsistency Paul vigorously rebuked

1. Read Galatians 2:11-16.
2. Verse 12:
   - (a) Where had Peter before this time eaten with Gentiles?
   - (b) What was his defence when criticised on that occasion?
   - (c) Why did he not at this time offer the same defence?
   - (d) From the conduct of Peter as narrated in to-day's lesson it is clear that Peter had not entirely overcome his vacillation. What examples of impulsiveness and vacillation in the character of Peter are given in the gospels?
3. Verses 12 and 13: These verses show how deep-seated were the prejudices of the Christian Jews against associating on an equality with Gentile converts. Barnabas, who had witnessed the reception of the Gospel among the Gentiles, was himself carried away by the influence of Jewish exclusiveness. In spite of the ruling of the council at Jerusalem, the Judaizing party within the Church was not silenced. This party constantly opposed the work of Paul; again and again he met their arguments with keen and incisive logic.
4. Verse 14: How do you account for the boldness of Paul in rebuking Peter?
5. There was no violent break, as some think, in consequence of this occurrence at Antioch. Peter speaks affectionately of Paul in one of his letters. See 2 Peter 3:15.

Thought for the Day: Are you, too, ever guilty of inconsistent conduct? Do you act and say one thing when among Christians and quite another thing when among those who are not Christians? Are you ready to blame Peter for his action, but slow to condemn yourself for equal inconsistency?

PART V

Paul's Second Missionary Journey

Study XII.—From Antioch to Philippi
Study XIII.—From Philippi to Athens
Study XIV.—From Athens to Antioch

Study XII.—From Antioch to Philippi
First Day: Paul and Silas Go Through Syria and Cilicia

After no long stay in Antioch Paul started out on his second missionary journey. On this tour Silas, instead of Barnabas, accompanied him. Leaving the city of Antioch, Paul and Silas passed through Syria and Cilicia, confirming the churches.

1. Read Acts 15:36-41.
2. How much time is indicated by the "some days after" of verse 36? A short or long space of time? See page 51, section 5.
3. What relationship existed between Barnabas and John Mark? Colossians 4:10.
4. Why did John Mark leave them in Pamphylia? See page 69, section 4.
5. In verse 39, the word "contention" (or "sharp contention," R.V.) is the translation of the Greek word παροξυσμός (*paroxysmos*), which appears in English in the word *paroxysm*. It indicates a sharp contention which soon subsides. We should not think that after this event Paul and Barnabas were estranged from each other. In his *First Epistle to the Corinthians*, written four or five years after the date of to-day's lession, Paul speaks of Barnabas on terms of perfect equality with himself.
6. As a result of this contention between Paul and Barnabas two pairs of missionaries, instead of one, went out to preach. The event seems not to have been without its influence upon Mark, for Paul subsequently found him a valuable helper. See 2 Timothy 4:11.
7. (a) When were the churches of Syria founded?
   (b) When and by whom were the churches of Cilicia founded?
   (c) Have you marked any city in Cilicia with a cross on your map?

THOUGHT FOR TO-DAY: We may honestly differ from one another on matters of policy, and even on questions of morals and religion, but we should never let our differences embitter us. By working from different points of view toward the same end, men contribute more richly to the final result.

Study XII.—From Antioch to Philippi
Second Day: Paul at Derbe and Lystra

From Cilicia, Paul and Silas passed into Lycaonia, to the towns of Derbe and Lystra. At Lystra Paul found Timothy, whom he took with him on leaving that city. Paul, Silas, and Timothy then journeyed through the neighboring cities, delivering the decree voted by the apostles and elders at Jerusalem.

1. Read Acts 16:1-5.
2. What inference do you draw from verse 2?
3. Construct a picture of the home life of Timothy from the following verses found in one of Paul's letters:
   (a) 2 Timothy 3:15.
   (b) 2 Timothy 1:5.
4. Verse 3: Timothy, although his father was a Greek, would be considered a Jew because he was the son of a Jewish mother. Timothy, however, had never been circumcised, and as an uncircumcised Jew was particularly unacceptable to other Jews, Paul circumcised him. This would make no difference to the Gentiles, and would not infringe upon the spirit of the Jerusalem decree, since that decree applied only to Gentiles.
5. To what influences do you ascribe the growth in faith and increase in numbers of the churches mentioned in verse 5?

Thought for the Day: It is a great thing to know when to yield to the opinion of others. Paul, in the circumcision of Timothy, without surrendering any of his principles, yielded to the prejudices of the Jews. Similarly we, whenever possible, should be willing, for the sake of peace and for the extension of the kingdom of God, to concede something to others, provided, of course, we do not give up any of our moral principles. When we stand out against others we should be sure that we do so from principle and not from pride.

Study XII.—**From Antioch to Philippi**

Third Day: Paul Has a Vision: He Goes over into Macedonia

In the providence of God the time had now come for the spread of the Gospel in Europe. Paul and his helpers, after preaching in the cities of Lycaonia, traveled through Phrygia and Galatia. When they reached Troas in northwest Asia Minor, Paul had a vision in which a man of Macedonia begged him to come over into Macedonia. At once Paul crossed from Asia into Europe, and came to the important city of Philippi.

1. Read Acts 16:6-12.
2. Verse 6: The word *Asia* in the New Testament is used always as the name of the Roman province of Asia—a district including the greater part of western Asia Minor. For its extent, see map, page 64.
3. Verses 6-8: The route of Paul is given clearly by Ramsay as follows: "Paul and his companions made a progress through the Phrygian *Region* of the province of Galatia, and then crossed the frontier of the province of Asia; but here they were prevented from preaching, and the prohibition was made absolute for the entire province. They therefore kept to the north across Asian Phrygia with the intention of entering the adjoining Roman province, Bithynia; but when they came opposite Mysia and were attempting to go out of Asia into Bithynia, the spirit of Jesus suffered them not. They therefore kept on towards the west through Mysia, without preaching in it (as it was part of Asia) until they came out on its western coast at the great harbour of Troas."
4. Mark Galatian Phrygia with a cross on your outline map.
5. Verse 10: From the "we" of this verse it is inferred that Luke, the writer of Acts, joined Paul's party at Troas.
6. Troas was on the coast of Mysia, not far from Ilium, the scene of the Trojan war.

Thought for the Day: From verses 6, 7, and 10 of to-day's lesson, it is clear that the apostles gave themselves up completely to the sway of the Holy Spirit. Are you willing to be so guided and directed for useful service?

Study XII.—From Antioch to Philippi
Fourth Day: The Gospel in Philippi

The first converts in Philippi were women. One of these, Lydia by name, hospitably opened her home to Paul and his company.

1. Read Acts 16:12-15.
2. Philippi was an important city of Macedonia, situated about ten miles from the sea. Augustus made it a "colony" after his victory over Brutus and Cassius in 42 B.C. Its inhabitants had Roman citizenship, they could vote in the Roman tribes, they had their own senate and magistrates, and used the Roman law and language.
3. Mark Philippi with a cross upon your outline map.
4. Apparently there was no synagogue in Philippi. The Jewish women met outside the city for prayer upon the banks of the Gangites. There they were free from interruption, and could use the waters of the river in their ablutions.
5. Where was the city of Thyatira? What importance did this city have in the Church at a later time?
6. Verse 14: Paul's first convert in Europe was a woman. Lydia was doubtless a proselyte, and so was found among the Jewish women who worshipped by the river-side; that she was a woman of means is clear from the fact that she was able to take Paul and his helpers into her house.
7. How many persons can you name who accompanied Paul at this time, and who are included in the pronoun "us" of verse 15?
8. Christianity brought a more honorable position to women than they had had, and gave them greater freedom.

"This is the first example of that family religion to which Paul so often refers in his Epistles. First came the faith of Lydia, then her leading all around her to Christ, then their baptismal confession, then her love evidenced in pressing hospitality, finally her receiving into her house Paul and Silas after their discharge from prison; she was not 'ashamed of the Lord's prisoners, but was a partaker of the afflictions of the gospel.'"

Study XII.—From Antioch to Philippi
Fifth Day: Paul Casts Out an Evil Spirit: Paul and Silas Are Imprisoned

One day while in Philippi, Paul cast an evil spirit out of a girl who practiced soothsaying. When her masters saw that they could no longer make money from her soothsaying, they brought Paul and Silas into court, stirred up a mob against them, and had them beaten and imprisoned.

1. Read Acts 16:16-24.
2. It is impossible to determine with what species of mental or spiritual trouble the girl was afflicted. Luke, an intelligent and educated man, calls it "a spirit of divination."
3. Verse 18: Why was Paul grieved at the words of the girl? Was not her statement a true one?
4. Verse 20: The "magistrates" were the two Roman prætors.
5. From verses 20 and 21 it would seem that the masters of the girl were Greeks. They were anxious to impress upon the Roman judge their loyalty to Roman rule, in order to gain his influence against Paul and Silas.
6. Verse 22: It was always easy at that time to stir up a mob against the Jews, just as is also the case nowadays in some countries.
7. In verse 22 the R.V. reads: "commanded to beat them with rods." These were the rods of the Roman lictors. Paul alludes to this beating in 2 Corinthians 11:25.
8. Paul was a Roman citizen, and should not have been beaten before his condemnation. The question therefore arises why he did not appeal to his rights as a Roman citizen. The following reasons may be given:
   (a) The trial, which seems to have been incomplete and irregular, may have been carried on in Latin, and of this language Paul and Silas may have been ignorant.
   (b) Roman prætors were sometimes cruel and merciless. Cicero tells how Verres, a Roman governor in Sicily, scourged a Roman citizen, though in the midst of his agony he kept exclaiming: *"Civis Romanus sum"* ("I am a Roman citizen.")

Thought for the Day: The masters of the girl out of whom the spirit of divination was cast prosecuted Paul because of their love of money. What does Paul say about the love of money? See 1 Timothy 6:9 and 10.

Study XII.—From Antioch to Philippi
Sixth Day: Conversion of the Jailer and His Family

Paul and Silas were unable to sleep in the jail at Philippi; they were fastened in stocks which allowed them no change of position, and their backs were sore and bleeding from the cruel beating they had suffered. To while away the hours of the night they prayed and sang hymns; an earthquake opened the prison doors, and the jailer and his family were converted through the exhortation of the apostles.

1. Read Acts 16:25-34.
2. Verse 25: "The prisoners were listening to them." The Greek verb here translated, "listening," is not the common one for "hearing." It denotes careful hearkening. In what language did Paul and Silas sing?
3. Paul in certain of his letters urges the Christians to sing: see Ephesians 5:19; Colossians 3:16.
4. Earthquakes are frequent in Greece. An earthquake shock might easily unhinge doors, and release prisoners chained to walls.
5. Verse 27: Why was the jailer about to kill himself?
6. What causes led the jailer to ask the question, "What must I do to be saved"? Did he assign the extraordinary events of the night to the influence of Paul and Silas? Do you think that he knew anything about Paul's preaching?
7. Read again slowly the lesson of to-day, Acts 16:25-34, and let your imagination picture to you the whole scene.

Memory Verse: Read and memorize Acts 4:12.

Prayer: "O God, let the sighing of the prisoner come before Thee, and mercifully grant unto us that we may be delivered by Thine almighty power from all bonds and chains of sin whether in our bodies or in our souls, through Jesus Christ our Lord." *Amen.*

Study XII.—From Antioch to Philippi
Seventh Day: The Release of Paul and Silas

On the morrow after the imprisonment of Paul and Silas, the magistrates, learning that they were Roman citizens, came to the prison and besought them to leave the city. Paul and Silas entered into the house of Lydia, greeted the brethren, and then departed from Philippi.

1. Read Acts 16:35-40.
2. The word "sergeants" (verse 35) is the translation of a Greek word which means "rod-bearers" or "lictors." These lictors were the attendants of the prætors.
3. Verse 38: Why did the magistrates fear? What had they done that was illegal?
4. From verses 37 and 38 it is clear that Silas, like Paul, was a Roman citizen.
5. Luke does not use the pronoun "we" in verse 40, nor does it appear again until Acts 20:6. From these two passages it is inferred that Luke remained in Philippi, or in that region at least, until Paul came again on his way to Jerusalem during his third missionary journey.
6. The Church at Philippi was always especially fond of Paul. On four different occasions they sent him gifts for his support: Philippians 4:10 and 4:16; 2 Corinthians 11:9.
7. Read rapidly in review the introductory paragraphs of each lesson in this week's work (*Study XII*).

"Thus the first chapter of the work to which the Lord had called them by a vision came to an end. Thus far it had been a work of peculiar suffering and of apparently small fruitage. But the future was to give abundant proof that their coming to Philippi had indeed been of the Lord."—*Gilbert.*

Study XIII.—From Philippi to Athens

First Day: Paul Preaches in Thessalonica

From Philippi Paul and his companions journeyed westward until they came to Thessalonica, the capital of the Roman province of Macedonia. Here Paul's labors were very successful. His converts seem to have been Gentiles chiefly.

1. Read Acts 17:1-4.
2. For the route of Paul through Philippi, through Amphipolis and Apollonia, see the map, page 64. Mark both Amphipolis and Apollonia on your outline map with crosses.
3. The Ignatian Way (*Via Ignatia*) ran from Philippi through Amphipolis and Apollonia to Thessalonica. Over this road Paul journeyed.
4. Thessalonica was situated on the Thermaic Gulf. Its harbor and its position on the Ignatian Way gave it great advantages in commerce; it was the administrative center, or capital, of the Roman province of Macedonia, and contained a large Jewish population.
5. Verse 2: For Paul's practice of preaching first in the synagogues of the Jews, see Acts 13:5 and 14; and 14:1.
6. From verse 4 may be learned an important fact: In many cities Greeks of the upper class were accustomed to attend the services of the synagogue, attracted thither, doubtless, by the simplicity and earnestness of the worship as compared with the rites of the heathen temples. The "devout Greeks" were probably proselytes.
7. More Greeks than Jews seem to have been converted (verse 4). This is clear also from one of Paul's letters: see 1 Thessalonians 1:9 and 2:14.
8. Mark Thessalonica with a cross upon your outline map.

"The synagogue audience [in Thessalonica] was mainly composed of Jews, and of these some were converted and joined the Church. . . . A larger number, however, of proselytes and of Greeks accepted the faith, and not a few women, of whom some were in a leading position. The inveterate obstinacy of the Jews, contrasting sadly with the ready conversion of the Gentiles, is a phenomenon which constantly recurs in the early history of Christianity. The Jew was at least in the possession of a religion which had raised him to a height of moral superiority above his Gentile contemporaries; but the Gentile of this day had no religion at all worth speaking of."—*Canon Farrar.*

Study XIII.—From Philippi to Athens
Second Day: Paul Preaches in Thessalonica (Continued)

Paul, in a letter to the Thessalonians written not long after this time, gives an account of the manner in which he worked and preached while among them. The details are interesting because from them it can be learned how Paul conducted himself in Gentile cities during his missionary tours.

1. Paul supported himself by working at his trade. See 1 Thessalonians 2:9. What was his trade?
2. "One of the staple manufactures of the city was and is goat's-hair cloth. The sound that follows the ear as one walks through the streets of Saloniki (Thessalonica) to-day is the wheezing and straining vibration of the loom and the pendulum-like click of the regular and ceaseless shuttle."
3. Yet Paul's labor seems not to have produced enough for his support: See Philippians 4:16.
4. Paul taught that men should support themselves by honest labor: 2 Thessalonians 3:7-10.
5. His preaching was sincere; his aim was unselfish; he sought to please God rather than man: 1 Thessalonians 2:1-8.
6. His preaching was effectual: 1 Thess. 1:5 and 6.

LESSON THOUGHT: Paul's two letters to the Thessalonians, which will be studied later, enable us to learn not a little concerning the advice and instruction which he gave his Gentile converts. In particular, three verses in First Thessalonians seem to sum up the cheerful, positive, and helpful exhortation of the apostle: Memorize 1 Thess. 5:16-18.

Study XIII.—From Philippi to Athens
Third Day: The Unbelieving Jews Stir Up a Mob

The unbelieving Jews of Thessalonica, angered because Paul, after a few weeks of preaching, had been more successful than they in making converts among the Gentiles, gathered a mob and assaulted the house of Jason, Paul's host. Jason was taken before the magistrates, but was later released on bail.

1. Read Acts 17:5-9.
2. Verse 5: What do you infer from this verse regarding the influence of the Jews in the city of Thessalonica?
3. The "rulers of the city" were the seven politarchs.
4. From verse 6 it is apparent that news of the spread of the Gospel in other parts of the Roman world had reached Thessalonica.
5. Verses 6 and 7: Do you think that the men composing this mob were sincere in their zeal for the authority of Cæsar?
6. Who was the Cæsar, or Roman Emperor, at this time? For the date of these events see the chronological outline, page xi.
7. Thessalonica, though a free city, was subject to the Roman Emperor. Why were the rulers of the city troubled? Had anything unlawful been done?
8. For the fear which the authorities of Greek towns had of the Roman government, see the words of the town clerk of Ephesus after a riot like this one had taken place at Ephesus: Acts 19:35-40.

"The success of Paul in Thessalonica, though his work was broken off by persecution, was very great. The Thessalonians received his word as the word of God and rejoiced in the midst of afflictions. They soon became an example to all believers in the provinces of Macedonia and Achaia, and their Christian life was everywhere known (see 1 Thess. 1:6-8). Paul was tenderly attached to them, and esteemed them as his joy and crown of glorying (Thess. 2:19 and 20)."—*Gilbert.*

Study XIII.—From Philippi to Athens

Fourth Day: Paul Goes to Berea: Flees Thence to Athens

The danger of injury to the apostle Paul was so great that the Christians of Thessalonica sent him off by night to Berea. At Berea Paul preached the Gospel with marked success. Learning of this, the Jews of Thessalonica came to Berea and stirred up the people. Thereupon the disciples of Berea sent Paul away to Athens. Timothy and Silas remained at Berea.

1. Read Acts 17:10-15.
2. Locate Berea and mark it with a cross.
3. What reason do you assign for the receptive attitude of the Bereans?
4. In verse 12 who are designated by the words "many of them"? Who are the honorable women? See Acts 13:50 and the note on that verse, page 74, section 2.
5. Verse 14: The reading of the R.V. is to be preferred here: "the brethren sent forth Paul to go as far as the sea."
6. Berea was the last town of Macedonia in which Paul preached on this tour. While in Macedonia he had preached in Philippi, Thessalonica, and Berea; whether he visited other towns cannot be known. His work influenced the entire province; for shortly after this he wrote to the Thessalonians that the Gospel was known throughout all Macedonia: See 1 Thess. 1:8.
7. Athens in the days of St. Paul had no great political importance, for Corinth was the Roman capital of Achaia. But Athens was still the intellectual center of Greece; its schools of philosophy were famous; it had beautiful temples adorned with precious works of art; the traditions of its ancient greatness were still powerful, and to it the world turned for culture and polish.

Two schools of philosophy, mentioned in the New Testament, were prominent at Athens at this time—the Epicurean and the Stoic. The Epicureans believed that the highest good was pleasure; not sensual pleasure, but rather a state in which the mind was free from care and the body from pain. The Stoics held that the highest good was virtue. Virtue depended upon knowledge, and knowledge could come only through the senses. Man's life was bound up with the universe. He must bring himself into harmony with the universe; he must suffer proudly and in silence.

Study XIII.—From Philippi to Athens
Fifth Day: Paul's Labors at Athens

Timothy soon joined Paul at Athens, but Paul, anxious for the welfare of the Thessalonian Church, sent him to Thessalonica. Silas probably still remained at Berea. While waiting for them to rejoin him, Paul was moved by the idolatry of Athens, and began to preach in the synagogue and teach in the market-place (*agora*). Certain of the philosophers of the city took him to the Areopagus (Hill of Ares), and asked him to explain more fully the strange doctrines he was teaching.

1. Paul at this time greatly wished to visit Thessalonica: See 1 Thess. 2:17 and 18. Timothy, on coming to Athens, was dispatched to Thessalonica: 1 Thess. 3:1-5.
2. Read Acts 17:16-21.
3. Verse 16, Revised Version: "Now, while Paul waited for them at Athens his spirit was provoked within him, as he beheld the city *full of idols*." Pausanias, a Greek traveler not long after Paul's time, says that there were more statues in Athens than in all the rest of Greece together. A Roman writer says, in referring to the statues in Athens, that it was easier to meet a god than a man.
4. Verse 17: How would the arguments differ which Paul used in the synagogue and in the market-place?
5. The Epicureans believed that the gods did not care for the world, but dwelt apart in perfect happiness. The Stoics held that God had produced the universe and that it would some day be absorbed by Him. What were some of the other beliefs of the Epicureans and the Stoics?
6. "Babbler" (verse 18) is the imperfect translation of a Greek word which means "seed-gatherer." It may have been a slang term used at Athens to designate those who picked up scraps of knowledge.
7. The Areopagus (Hill of Ares, or Mars Hill) was a small hill west of the Acropolis. On this hill the Court of the Areopagus used to meet. In full view were the splendid buildings of the Acropolis and of the city.

A love of knowledge for its own sake was a marked characteristic of the Greeks: See 1 Corinthians 1:22. The Athenians were especially noted for their busy intellectual curiosity and for an inveterate desire to talk, dispute, and argue.

Study XIII.—From Philippi to Athens
Sixth Day: Paul's Sermon on the Areopagus

Standing on the Areopagus, with the splendid statues, shrines, and temples of the city in full view, surrounded by an audience composed of Epicureans, Stoics, and idlers of the market-place, St. Paul preached the sermon contained in Acts 17:22-31.

1. Read Acts 17:22-28.
2. In verse 22 the Greek word rendered in the A.V. "too superstitious," and in the R.V. "somewhat superstitious," means rather: "unusually religious." Paul was a tactful man, and would naturally begin by conciliating his audience.
3. Verse 23: The R.V. has "the objects of your worship" for "your devotions" of the A.V.
4. The inscription was TO AN UNKNOWN GOD or TO UNKNOWN GOD. Greek writers tell of altars at Athens dedicated *to gods unknown*. Probably the Athenians, in their desire to please the deities, had erected them on spots where strange or supernatural events had taken place.
5. Verse 24: Is there any reason why Paul should allude to *temples* in this verse?
6. The Greeks called all non-Greeks "barbarians," and regarded them as ignorant and uncivilized. But Paul in verse 26 preaches the brotherhood of man.
7. The quotation "For we are his offspring" is found in the writings of Aratus of Soli (in Cilicia), who flourished about 275 B.C. The same words are also found in the poems of Cleanthes, who was a native of Assos in Asia Minor. He lived in the third century B.C. When did Paul become acquainted with the Greek poets?

THOUGHT FOR THE DAY: The introduction of Paul's address is marked by great tact and courtesy. He does not rebuke them sharply for their idolatry, nor call them to account sternly for their neglect of duty. He begins by saying that the Athenians are unusually religious: they even erect an altar *to an unknown god* so as to include all divinities; he then declares the unknown God to be the Lord of Heaven, who created all men to love and serve Him. Men are His children, even as the Greek poets have said.

Study XIII.—From Philippi to Athens
Seventh Day: Paul's Sermon on the Areopagus (Continued)

By means of his tactful introduction, Paul conciliated his audience and gained their attention. He then went on to preach Jesus and the Resurrection. When he mentioned the resurrection of the dead, the Athenians mocked at him; nevertheless, a few of them believed and were converted.

1. Read Acts 17:29-34.
2. State in your own words, supplying any missing sentences, the argument of verse 29.
3. Why did the doctrine of the resurrection prove to be unacceptable to the Athenians?
4. Paul's work in Athens was not altogether a failure. Dionysius, the Areopagite, must have been a man of influence, since members of the Court of the Areopagus were at least sixty years of age, and had filled important offices of the city. Tradition says that Dionysius was the first bishop of Athens. Of Damaris nothing is known.
5. The Athenians were too exclusive, too frivolous, and too much wrapped up in their own conceits to readily embrace the Gospel. It is not recorded that Paul ever visited them again. No *Epistle to the Athenians* is even mentioned. Paul may have had the Athenians in mind when he wrote: "Be not wise in your own conceits." (Romans 12:16.)
6. Mark Athens with a cross on your outline map.

Lesson Thought: "For the word of the cross, to those in the way of perdition, is folly; but to us in the way of salvation, it is the power of God. And so it is written, *I will destroy the wisdom of the wise, and bring to nothing the understanding of the prudent.* Where is the Philosopher? Where is the Rabbi? Where is the reason of this world? Has not God turned the world's wisdom into folly? for when the world had failed to gain by its wisdom the knowledge of God in the wisdom of God, it pleased God, by the folly of our preaching, to save those who believe."—St. Paul, *First Corinthians* 15:18-21 (Conybeare and Howson's translation).

Study XIV.—From Athens to Antioch

First Day: Paul Goes to Corinth and Labors Among the Jews

Discouraged by the unfavorable reception that the Gospel had met with in Athens, Paul left that city and came to Corinth. He made his home with Aquila and Priscilla, who were tent-makers by occupation. While waiting for Timothy and Silas to come from Macedonia, Paul taught in the synagogue every Sabbath, preaching to Jews and to Greek proselytes.

1. Read Acts 18:1-4.
2. The Romans had divided all Greece into two provinces—Macedonia and Achaia. The capital of Macedonia was Thessalonica, the capital of Achaia was Corinth.
3. Corinth was situated on the isthmus connecting Central Greece and the Peloponnesus. Its location made it a city of great commercial importance; its wealth and its cosmopolitan population led to a lax state of morals; the worship of Aphrodite (Venus) was carried on with gross immorality.
4. Aquila and Priscilla were Roman Jews. What do the names *Aquila* and *Priscilla* mean?
5. Claudius expelled the Jews from Rome some time between 50 and 52 A.D. The Roman historian Suetonius says that this was done on account of Jewish tumults instigated by a person named Chrestus (i. e., Christus or Christ). From this testimony it is clear that the Jewish Christians in Rome had been attacked by their unbelieving brethren.
6. Paul apparently could not earn enough at this time for his support: See 2 Cor. 11:9.
7. Mark Corinth with a cross upon your outline map.

The Scenes of Corinth: How deeply Paul was affected by the scenes of the city of Corinth may be seen in the Corinthian Epistles. His illustrations are those chiefly drawn from the Gentile customs—the lovely stadium, in which he had looked with sympathy on the grace and swiftness of many a youthful athlete (1 Cor. 9:24); the boxing-matches (1 Cor. 9:26 and 27); the insulting vanity of a Roman triumph (2 Cor. 2:14-16); the long hair of effeminate dandies (1 Cor. 11:14); the shows of the theater (1 Cor. 4:9); the fading garland of Isthmian pine (1 Cor. 9:25).—*Adapted from Canon Farrar.*

Study XIV.—From Athens to Antioch

Second Day: Paul's First Epistle to the Thessalonians

While Paul was working among the Jews and proselytes in Corinth, Silas and Timothy came from Macedonia. Timothy brought Paul cheering news of the Church at Thessalonica. Thereupon Paul wrote his *First Epistle to the Thessalonians*.

1. Read 1 Thessalonians 3:6 and 7, and Acts 18:5.
2. Acts 15:5: "Paul was constrained by the word" (R.V.); that is, he felt impelled more than ever to preach the Gospel. He had cheering news from the Thessalonian Church, he had the presence and sympathy of Silas and Timothy, and he was relieved of the necessity of constant labor.
3. On learning of the faith and good works of the Thessalonians and of their patience under persecution, Paul wrote the letter known as *First Thessalonians*. It was addressed to all the disciples at Thessalonica. This letter shows the affection of St. Paul for his converts, his great desire to see them, his sympathy with them in their sufferings, and his fervent wish that they might have rich spiritual gifts.
4. Read *First Thessalonians*. Even if read slowly, less than ten minutes will be required for the entire Epistle.
5. From this letter much can be learned concerning the Thessalonian Church:
    (a) Was the Church composed chiefly of Jews or of Gentiles?
    (b) What was the influence of the Church?
    (c) What sufferings had befallen them?
    (d) They were anxious about the second coming of Christ. What does Paul say about this second coming?

The Second Coming: Many of the early Christians believed that Christ would return to earth with power and glory in their own generation; little by little they came to see that the prophetic words as to His return referred rather to the passing away of the Jewish dispensation and the gradual growth of the Kingdom of God—the beginning of the last great period in God's dealings with man.

Study XIV.—**From Athens to Antioch**

Third Day: Paul Labors Among the Gentiles at Corinth

Strengthened and helped by the presence of Silas and Timothy, Paul preached among the Jews of Corinth with great power. When some of the unbelieving Jews opposed him, and blasphemed the Gospel, Paul abandoned his work among his fellow-countrymen, and turned to the Gentiles. No slight danger seems to have threatened Paul at this time, for the Lord appeared to him in a vision, and bade him banish his fear of injury.

1. Read Acts 18:5-11.
2. Paul's first converts at Corinth: 1 Corinthians 16:15; Acts 18:8. These first converts Paul himself baptized: 1 Cor. 1:14-16; many of the Corinthian converts were of humble rank: 1 Cor. 1:26.
3. Paul's gospel: At Athens Paul had spoken to please his Athenian audience, touching on the philosophy of religion and quoting the Greek poets; at Corinth he determined to preach in a more direct manner: See 1 Cor. 2:1-4, and 1 Cor. 1:17 and 18.
4. Paul's depression of mind while at Corinth: See 1 Cor. 2:3.
5. Paul's reassuring vision: Acts 18:9 and 10. Why was this vision sent Paul? A literal translation of the latter part of verse 9 would be: "Keep on speaking, do not be silent for a minute."
6. The "year and six months" of verse 11 probably fell within the years 52 to 54 A.D.

"How sweetly flowed the Gospel's sound
From lips of gentleness and grace,
While listening thousands gathered round,
And joy and gladness filled the place!

"Come, wanderers, to my Father's home;
Come, all ye weary ones, and rest.
Yes, sacred Teacher, we will come,
Obey Thee, love Thee, and be blest."
—*John Bowring.*

STUDY XIV.—From Athens to Antioch

FOURTH DAY: PAUL'S SECOND EPISTLE TO THE THESSALONIANS

In his *First Epistle to the Thessalonians* Paul had spoken of the second coming of Christ as near at hand. Influenced by this, some of the Thessalonians ceased to work, neglected their every-day duties, and gave themselves up to religious enthusiasm. To correct this tendency, St. Paul wrote his *Second Epistle to the Thessalonians,* in which he shows them what things must take place before Christ comes the second time.

1. What did Paul say in First Thessalonians regarding the second coming of Christ? See 1 Thess. 5:1-3, and 4:13-18.
2. Read 2 Thessalonians, chapter 2.
3. In the chapter just read Paul seeks to allay the fears of the Thessalonians concerning the second coming of Christ. What he means, however, is not clear, for his language is very guarded. He had, while with them, given more definite information (2 Thess. 2:5). Various conjectures have been made regarding the "man of sin, the son of perdition" (verse 3). St. Augustine says, "I confess I am entirely ignorant what the Apostle meant." One theory is that the Roman Emperor was the son of perdition whom Paul had in mind. Some Protestants have held that it was the Pope: some Catholics that it was Martin Luther.
4. Some one seems to have forged a letter over Paul's name, and to have sent it to the Thessalonians: 2 Thess. 2:2. Consequently Paul, who apparently always employed an amanuensis to write his letters, from this time forth adds in his own handwriting a few lines to each of his epistles as a sign of authenticity. See 2 Thess. 3:17; 1 Cor. 16:21; Galatians 6:11; Colossians 4:18.

THOUGHT FOR THE DAY: Are you willing that the Spirit of God should come into your heart and dwell there? Are you anxious that His Kingdom should now include you? Are you willing to put from you those things that might keep the Heavenly Guest from entering into your soul?

Study XIV.—From Athens to Antioch
Fifth Day: A Mob Attacks Paul at Corinth

Certain of the unbelieving Jews of Corinth, angered because of Paul's successful work among the Gentiles, stirred up a mob, and brought him before the Roman proconsul on the charge that he was teaching an unlawful religion. The proconsul contemptuously dismissed the case, whereupon the Greeks seized the ringleader of the Jews, and gave him a beating.

1. Read Acts 18:12-17.
2. What was the real reason which led the Jews to stir up persecution against Paul?
3. Gallio, the proconsul of Achaia, was the brother of the philosopher Seneca, and uncle of the poet Lucan. "He was the very flower of pagan courtesy and pagan culture—a Roman with all a Roman's dignity and seriousness, and yet with all the grace and versatility of a polished Greek."
4. Verse 13: The Jewish law is meant by "the law" of this verse. Throughout the Roman Empire the Jewish religion was a *religio licita,* or lawful religion. The Jews of Corinth tried to persuade Gallio that the Christian religion was a spurious imitation of their own religion, and hence a *religio illicita,* or unlawful religion.
5. Verses 14 and 15: Gallio shows that he understands perfectly the Jewish fondness for idle discussions of the Jewish law. He was probably in Rome at the time when Claudius expelled the Jews. See Acts 18:2.
6. Verse 17: The Jews were unpopular among the Gentiles in St. Paul's time. It was always easy to stir up a mob against them; Jew-baiting was not uncommon. The contemptuous manner in which the proconsul dismissed the case was the signal for the lively Greeks to attack Sosthenes and give him a beating.
7. "And Gallio cared for none of these things." Perhaps he thought that the informal punishment of Sosthenes would be a valuable lesson.

Prayer: "O Lord, in whom is the truth, help us, we entreat Thee, to speak the truth in love, to hate a lie, to eschew exaggeration, inaccuracy, affectation. Yea, though tribulation or persecution should arise for the Truth's sake, suffer us not to be offended." *Amen.*

Study XIV.—From Athens to Antioch

Sixth Day: Paul Returns from Corinth to Antioch by Way of Ephesus

After laboring for many months in Corinth, Paul at last left the city to return to Antioch in Syria. On the voyage he stopped at Ephesus for a few days. From Ephesus he sailed to Cæsarea. From Cæsarea he went up to Jerusalem and greeted the Church, then proceeded overland to Antioch.

1. Read Acts 18:18-22.
2. Verse 18:
    (a) How long had Paul been in Corinth prior to the event of yesterday's lesson? See verse 11.
    (b) Who were Aquila and Priscilla?
    (c) Locate Cenchreæ.
    (d) Paul had taken upon himself the vow of a Nazarite: see Numbers 6:1-21. Paul, as is seen from to-day's lesson, did not abandon all of the Jewish rites and ceremonies. However, he held that they were not necessary for salvation.
3. Locate Ephesus, and mark it with a cross. From verses 19-21 nothing can be learned concerning the success of Paul's labors during his brief stay in Ephesus, save that the Jews desired him to remain longer.
4. Verse 22: Of this visit to Jerusalem nothing is known.
5. Verse 22: At Antioch Paul must have received a warm and enthusiastic welcome. Judging from Acts 14:27, what did Paul do immediately upon his return to Antioch?
6. In what cities had Paul preached during this second missionary journey?

Thought for the Day: After his return from Greece to Antioch the wickedness of Corinth seems still to have weighed heavily upon Paul's heart, for in the *Epistle to the Galatians,* written at Antioch, Paul speaks in particular of the "lusts of the flesh." Read carefully Galatians 5:16-21, and ask yourself whether any of these sins have dominion over you. Pray Him that you may have strength to resist them.

STUDY XIV.—From Athens to Antioch
SEVENTH DAY: PAUL WRITES THE EPISTLE TO THE GALATIANS

After his return to Antioch, Paul learned that certain Judaizing Christians had been at work among his Galatian converts, teaching them that they must be circumcised and must keep the Mosaic Law. These teachers sought to increase their own influence by alleging that Paul was not a genuine apostle since he had not seen the Lord Jesus, and had not derived his commission from the apostles at Jerusalem.

To vindicate his authority as an apostle, and to show that the law of Moses was not binding upon Christians, Paul wrote his *Epistle to the Galatians.*

1. Who were the Galatians? See page 79, section 4.
2. Paul's authority as an apostle: Galatians 1:1.
3. Paul's independence:
    (a) The source of his gospel: Gal. 1:11 and 12.
    (b) His relation to the apostles at Jerusalem: Gal. 1:15-20 and Gal. 2:1-10.
4. The fickleness of the Galatians and their desertion to Judaism: Gal. 1:6-9; 4:9-11.
5. The Law was preparatory to the coming of Christ: Gal. 4:1-8.
6. Faith in Christ, not the law, brings righteousness: Gal. 5:1-6.
7. Review rapidly the lessons of this Study (XIV) by reading the introductory paragraph of each.

THOUGHT FOR TO-DAY: In the *Epistle to the Galatians,* over against the "lusts of the flesh," noticed yesterday, Paul puts the "fruits of the Spirit." Read Galatians 5:22-26, and ask yourself whether you are trying to show these fruits of the Spirit.

PART VI

Paul's Third Missionary Journey

Study XV.—From Antioch to Ephesus
Study XVI.—From Ephesus to Corinth
Study XVII.—Paul's Last Journey to Jerusalem

Study XV.—From Antioch to Ephesus

First Day: Paul Travels Through Galatia and Phrygia: Apollos Goes to Ephesus

After a stay of some little time in Ephesus, Paul started out on his third missionary journey; he passed through Galatia into Phrygia, his destination being Ephesus. Meanwhile Apollos, a learned and eloquent Jew of Alexandria, arrived at Ephesus and began to teach among the Jews. Apollos, however, was imperfectly instructed in Christianity, knowing only the baptism of John. Aquila and Priscilla, however, taught him what was lacking.

1. Read Acts 18:23.
   (a) Paul's route was doubtless similar to that on his second missionary journey: See Acts 15:40 and 41; 16:1-6.
   (b) Timothy was probably with Paul at this time, for the apostle seems never to have traveled alone.
2. Read Acts 18:24-28.
3. Alexandria, in Egypt, was founded by Alexander the Great in 332 B.C. Because of its location and its fine harbor it became one of the centers of trade between the east and west; it grew rapidly, and soon contained a large population of Egyptians, Greeks, and Jews. The city had many handsome buildings, among which were the Museum and the great library. The Jews of Alexandria were profoundly influenced by the literary atmosphere of the brilliant Greek city in which they lived, and were so much interested in Greek culture that they diligently studied the Old Testament Scriptures, seeking to find parallels and analogies between them and the writings of the Greek philosophers. With this kind of learning Apollos was saturated.
4. Verse 25: There were Jews here and there who had believed in the preaching of John, and had accepted the baptism of repentance, but as yet did not know the doctrine of salvation by faith nor of the gift of the Holy Spirit. Such was the spiritual condition of Apollos.
5. When did Aquila and Priscilla (verse 26) come to Ephesus? Acts 18:2.
6. What part of Greece was designated as Achaia? What was the capital of Achaia?

Study XV.—From Antioch to Ephesus
Second Day: Paul Arrives at Ephesus

When Paul reached Ephesus, Apollos was already in Corinth. At Ephesus Paul found several disciples, who, like Apollos, knew only of the baptism of John. These men, after Paul had taught them, and had laid his hands on them, received the Holy Spirit.

1. Read Acts 19:1-7.
2. Verse 1: Had Paul been in Ephesus before? At what time, and how long did he stay? Acts 18:19 and 20.
3. Ephesus was the capital of the Roman province of Asia, which consisted of Mysia, Lydia, and Caria—the greater part of western Asia Minor. Ephesus was also the religious center of Asia Minor, for in it was the famous temple of Artemis, or Diana, which was one of the seven wonders of the world. This temple contained an image of Artemis, which fell down from heaven (Acts 19:35), also art treasures of immense value. The Ephesians were notorious for their belief in magical arts and for the use of amulets of parchment inscribed with incantations.
4. Paul now begins a long and eventful period of labor in the capital of the Roman province of Asia. In what capitals has he already labored?
5. Verse 2: John and his first disciples were not ignorant of the baptism of the Holy Spirit, but they seem not to have understood its significance. See the words of John the Baptist in Mark 1:8 and John 1:32 and 33.
6. Verse 4: It would seem from this verse that the twelve men with whom Paul was speaking knew little or nothing about Jesus as the Messiah.

"Holy Ghost, with light divine
  Shine upon this heart of mine;
Chase the shades of night away,
  Turn my darkness into day.

"Holy Spirit, all divine,
  Dwell within this heart of mine;
Cast down every idol-throne,
  Reign supreme, and reign alone."
—*Andrew Reed.*

Study XV.—From Antioch to Ephesus

Third Day: Paul Withdraws from the Synagogue to the School of Tyrannus

For three months Paul taught in the synagogue, but meeting with opposition from the unbelieving Jews, he withdrew to a school building, in which he taught and preached for the next two years. From Ephesus the Gospel spread throughout the whole province of Asia. So mightily did the Spirit of God rest upon Paul that special miracles were wrought by his hands.

1. Read Acts 19:8-12.
2. Verse 9: Tyrannus was probably a Sophist, a teacher of rhetoric and philosophy. He would rent his building to any one whose teachings did not conflict with his own.
3. "Reasoning daily in the school of Tyrannus" (verse 9). There were many questions to discuss, not only the doctrines of Christianity, but the relation of pagan life to Christianity—questions about marriage and divorce, slavery, the use of meat offered to idols, etc.
4. Verse 10: Observe the thoroughness with which the Gospel is spread throughout Roman Asia. In this province were those seven churches of Asia to whom John wrote in *Revelation:* See Rev. 1:11. Paul himself may have founded all these churches with the exception of that in Laodicea: Col. 2:1. Locate these places on your outline map, and mark them with crosses.
5. Verses 11 and 12: Why were the miracles of St. Paul likely to attract special attention at Ephesus? See page 116, section 3.
6. Verse 12: The aprons mentioned in this verse Paul may have worn while working at his trade of tent-making.

PRAYER: "Help me, O Lord, that by devotion to Thee and by the sweetness and purity of my life, I may bring others to Thee, and thus, like the blessed Apostle St. Paul, aid in spreading the Kingdom on earth." *Amen.*

Study XV.—**From Antioch to Ephesus**

Fourth Day: The Ephesians Burn Their Books of Magic

In Ephesus, the city of magic and of wonders, certain Jewish exorcists, learning of Paul's miracles, undertook to make use of his name and that of Jesus in casting out evil spirits. The consequences were so disastrous to the exorcists that fear fell upon the Ephesians, and many of them who had patronized or practiced magic renounced their deeds and burnt their books.

1. Read Acts 19:13-20.
2. Verse 13: An exorcist is one who casts out evil spirits. These men probably professed to cure diseases by charms and incantations; their methods may have been somewhat like the "medicine-men" of the North American Indians.
3. Why did these exorcists make use of the names of Jesus and of Paul?
4. Verse 16: Only two of the sons of Sceva were concerned on this occasion. Note that the R.V. says "mastered both of them."
5. Verses 17-20:
    (a) Verse 18: Many of the converted Ephesians had apparently continued to patronize or practice sorcery, magic, and soothsaying, perhaps not realizing that there was any evil in such a course. They now are led to see the folly of such superstitious rites.
    (b) The Jews had magic formulas and receipts for incantations and exorcisms dating from the time of Solomon; the Ephesians had charms made up of the words written upon the crown, girdle, and feet of the statue of Artemis (or Diana). These were the *Ephesia grammata,* mentioned by ancient writers.
    (c) The "pieces of silver" were probably Greek *drachmae.* As the *drachma* was worth a little less than twenty cents, the value of the books was almost ten thousand dollars.

The Mystery of the Gospel: In his letter to the Ephesians, the people who made so much of magic and mystery, Paul has much to say concerning the "mystery of Christ" and the "mystery of the Gospel." Read Ephesians 3:1-12.

Study XV.—From Antioch to Ephesus
Fifth Day: Details of Paul's Work at Ephesus

Certain details of Paul's work at Ephesus may be gathered from incidental allusions in his *First Epistle to the Corinthians,* and from a speech delivered at Miletus to the elders of Ephesus, reported in Acts 20:17-36.

1. The field, its advantages and disadvantages: 1 Cor. 16:8 and 9.
2. The thoroughness of Paul's work: Acts 19:10 and 20:20.
3. Paul's doctrine: Acts 20:21.
4. His earnestness: Acts 20:31.
5. Paul worked at his trade: Acts 20:34; his reason for so doing: Acts 20:35.
6. At this time Paul may have suffered some of the hardships which he mentions in his two letters to the Corinthians: See 1 Cor. 4:9-13 and 2 Cor. 11:24-28.
7. Paul plans to visit Macedonia and Achaia; he sends two of his helpers on in advance: See Acts 19:21 and 22.
8. Acts 19:22: Erastus was a person of no little importance at Corinth: See Romans 16:23—an Epistle written at Corinth.

A Monument of Paul's Work: The most astonishing monument of the success of Paul's work at Ephesus is his *Epistle to the Ephesians.* "This is perhaps the profoundest book in existence; yet its author evidently expected the Ephesians to understand it. If the orations of Demosthenes, with their closely packed arguments, between whose articulations even a knife cannot be thrust, be a monument of the intellectual greatness of the Greece which listened to them with pleasure; if the plays of Shakespeare, with their deep views of life and their obscure and complex language, be a testimony to the strength of mind of the Elizabethan Age; then the Epistle to the Ephesians, which sounds the lowest depths of Christian doctrine and scales the loftiest heights of Christian experience, is a testimony to the proficiency which Paul's converts had attained under his preaching at Ephesus."—*Stalker.*

Study XV.—From Antioch to Ephesus
Sixth Day: Trouble in the Church at Corinth

During his sojourn of three years at Ephesus, Paul seems to have made a visit to Corinth not recorded by Luke in the book of Acts; he also wrote a letter to the Corinthians which is not extant. A little later Paul learned that there were factions in the Church at Corinth. About the same time, also, three men came from Corinth bearing a letter in which the Corinthians asked the Apostle for light on certain vexatious questions.

1. Paul's second visit to Corinth: Read 2 Cor. 13:1. Paul visited Corinth the first time on his second missionary journey. In the verse just read he says he is coming for the third time. The second visit was therefore made, in all likelihood, from Ephesus. Paul visited them "with sorrow": 2 Cor. 2:1 (R.V.). They had relapsed into heathen vice; he rebuked and warned them.
2. Paul's lost letter to the Corinthians: See 1 Cor. 5:9. This letter was written to correct the immoral tendencies of the Corinthians. It was sent, probably, soon after the visit mentioned in the paragraph above.
3. News of fresh trouble at Corinth:
   (a) Paul learns of factions in the Church: 1 Cor. 1:11.
   (b) A case of gross immorality: 1 Cor. 5:1.
   (c) Law-suits between Church members before pagan tribunals: 1 Cor. 6:1.
4. Three members of the Corinthian Church visit Paul: 1 Cor. 16:17. They probably brought the letter mentioned by Paul in 1 Cor. 7:1.
5. In the letter sent to Paul, the Corinthians ask Paul for advice on certain matters pertaining to moral conduct and to worship.

PAUL ON CHRISTIAN LOVE: Paul's cure for the factions and disorders of the Corinthian Church was *love*. Read the thirteenth chapter of First Corinthians. If you read the A.V. be sure to substitute throughout the chapter the word *love* for the word *charity*.

STUDY XV.—*From Antioch to Ephesus*
SEVENTH DAY: PAUL'S FIRST EPISTLE TO THE CORINTHIANS

Paul, on learning of the factions in the Church at Corinth and of the existence of gross immorality, now writes the letter known as *First Corinthians*. In this epistle he also answers the questions asked in the letter from Corinth—brought probably by Stephanas, Fortunatus, and Achaicus.

1. There were four factions at Corinth, consisting of the followers of Paul, Apollos, Cephas or Peter, and Christ. Paul had been liberal in the treatment of the questions arising between Jew and Gentile, hence Paul's party was the liberal faction; Apollos had captivated the Greeks with the philosophical turn which he gave his preaching: his party was the philosophical faction; Peter's party was the Judaizing faction; lastly, those who followed neither Paul nor Apollos nor Peter called themselves Christ's party.
2. For Paul's treatment of these factions, read 1 Cor. 1:10-24.
3. Paul's rebuke of gross immorality: 1 Cor. 5:1-5, and 9-11.
4. His advice to those who were fond of law-suits: 1 Cor. 6:1-7.
5. His advice concerning the observance of the Lord's Supper: 1 Cor. 11:20-30.
6. Paul also answers in this letter various questions asked him by the Corinthian Church: On marriage, on meat offered to idols, on the conduct of public worship, on the use of spiritual gifts.
7. He instructs the Corinthians to get ready a collection for the poor at Jerusalem: 1 Cor. 16:1-4.

MEAT OFFERED TO IDOLS: One of the questions that bothered some of the early Gentile Christians was that of meat offered to idols. In ancient sacrifice oftentimes only part of the victim was burned; the rest of the carcass was returned to the worshipper or given to the poor. Is it right, asked the Christians, to eat such meat? For St. Paul's answer read 1 Cor. chapter 8. The principle laid down by Paul in verses 9 to 13 is the one that should be kept in mind nowadays by those Christians who honestly differ regarding certain questions of amusement, the observance of the Sabbath day, etc.

Study XVI.—From Ephesus to Corinth
First Day: Paul's Troubles at Ephesus

Paul's troubles at Ephesus were twofold: on the one hand the immorality and disorder of the Corinthian Church deeply grieved him; on the other hand he was prostrated by a severe illness in which he almost despaired of life.

1. St. Paul sent Timothy to Corinth shortly before writing First Corinthians: See Acts 19:22 and 1 Cor. 4:17.
2. It is believed by some scholars that Timothy came back from Corinth to Ephesus bringing word that First Corinthians had not been received altogether with favor. Timothy seems to have been insulted or wronged by some one: 2 Cor. 7:11 and 12.
3. Grieved by the news brought by Timothy, St. Paul wrote a letter, which is not extant. This letter he wrote in much anguish of mind: 2 Cor. 2:3 and 4, and 2 Cor. 7:8. In this letter Paul urged that the wrongdoer be disciplined.
4. The letter was probably sent by Titus and an unknown brother: 2 Cor. 12:18.
5. Paul's illness: 2 Cor. 1:8 and 9. This illness was accompanied by persecution and anxiety: 2 Cor. 4:8-10, and 6:4 and 5.

"The terrible closing scenes at Ephesus, the revolt of Galatia and Corinth, and the prostrating attack of sickness by their concurrent effect brought Paul into the lowest depths of affliction, and God is now to him above all 'the Father of consolations.'"

St. Paul's Consolation: "Blessed be God, even the Father of our Lord Jesus Christ, the Father of mercies and the God of all comfort; who comforteth us in all our tribulation, that we may be able to comfort them which are in any trouble, by the comfort wherewith we ourselves are comforted of God. For as the sufferings of Christ abound in us, so our consolation also aboundeth by Christ."
—*Second Epistle to the Corinthians*, 1:3-5.

Study XVI.—From Ephesus to Corinth
Second Day: Paul is Opposed by a Shrine-Makers' Trade-Union

Owing to Paul's labors in Ephesus and neighboring cities, Christianity spread rapidly throughout the province of Asia. So many converts were gained from paganism that the tradesmen who sold silver shrines of Artemis (Diana) were aware of a marked decrease in business. Alarmed at this, the silversmiths held a meeting in order to take steps to counteract the teaching of Paul. The meeting soon became noisy and turbulent.

1. Read Acts 19:23-28.
2. Demetrius seems to have been a wholesale dealer in shrines of Artemis (or Diana). The influence of the great temple of Artemis at Ephesus had been very powerful up to this time, and the sale of shrines was a lucrative business. The "craftsmen" of verse 24 were skilled workmen who made the shrines.
3. Compare verse 26 with verse 10 of this same chapter.
4. It was now the month of May, a month devoted at Ephesus to the worship of Artemis, and hence named the Artemisian month. At this time the *Ephesia* was celebrated—a festival in honor of the goddess. To this festival vast throngs of pilgrims and visitors were accustomed to flock. Apparently, however, not so many came as usual, or else there was in other ways a lack of interest in the celebration, for the silversmiths were aware of a diminution in the sale of shrines.
5. Verse 27: Some years later, Pliny, the Roman governor of Bithynia, in a letter to the Emperor Trajan, wrote that owing to the spread of Christianity in Asia the temples were vacated, the pagan feasts were neglected, and victims for sacrifices could find no buyers.

Thought for the Day: Do men oppose Christianity at the present time because its teachings, if carried out in practice, cause a diminution of their business profits? Can you think of any forms of business in which Christians should not engage?

STUDY XVI.—From Ephesus to Corinth
THIRD DAY: THE SHRINE-MAKERS CAUSE A RIOT

The meeting of silversmiths and workmen who had gathered to oppose the work of Paul soon became so noisy that people came running from every quarter to learn the cause of the outcry. Maddened with religious fanaticism, the mob seized two of Paul's companions and carried them into the theater. So great was the uproar and confusion that the majority of those present did not know why they had come together.

1. Read Acts 19:29-34.
2. Verse 29:
    (a) Gaius is otherwise unknown; Aristarchus is mentioned several times subsequently; for his city and nationality, see Acts 27:2.
    (b) The theater at Ephesus would seat from twenty-five to thirty thousand people.
3. Why did Paul wish to go in to the people in the theater?
4. Verse 31: The "chief officers of Asia" were local officers in the cities of Asia in charge of the games and religious festivals of the province.
5. Verse 33: This was a riot directed primarily against the Christians, but as many of the Christians were Jews, the mob failed to discriminate between Christian and non-Christian Jews. So the non-Christian Jews in the theater put forward Alexander to explain that Jews were not Christians, though some Christians might happen to be renegade Jews.

"Alexander succeeded in struggling somewhere to the front, and stood before the mob with outstretched hand in the attempt to win an audience for his oration. But no sooner had the mob recognized the well-known traits of Jewish physiognomy than they vented their hate in a shout of 'Great is Artemis of the Ephesians!' . . . For two hours, as though they had been howling dervishes, did this mongrel Greek crowd continue incessantly their senseless yell. By that time they were sufficiently exhausted to render it possible to get a hearing."—*Canon Farrar.*

Study XVI.—From Ephesus to Corinth
Fourth Day: The Shrine-Makers' Riot (Continued)

For two hours the mob shouted its fanatical cry, "Great is Artemis of the Ephesians!" Then the town clerk quieted them, and by a wise and sensible speech led them to disperse.

1. Read Acts 19:35-41.
2. Notes on verse 35:
    (a) Town clerk: He was the recorder of the city, had charge of the archives, and made all public communications known to the city.
    (b) In this verse, as in verses 24, 27, 28, and 34, the Greek name *Artemis* should appear rather than the Latin *Diana*. Similarly, *Zeus* should be substituted for *Jupiter*.
    (c) The image fabled to have fallen from heaven was "a figure swathed like a mummy, covered with monstrous breasts, and holding in one hand a trident and in the other a club."
3. Verse 37:
    (a) The Jews were often accused of temple-robbing. See Romans 2:22 (R.V.).
    (b) From the latter part of this verse what do you infer regarding Paul's treatment of the worship of Artemis at Ephesus? How did Paul treat the pagan religion of Athens?
4. Verses 38-41:
    (a) The Greek word rendered "deputies" in the A.V. is correctly given as "proconsuls" in the R.V.
    (b) Verse 40 hints at fear of the Roman authorities. This was one of the occasions when the Roman power indirectly helped the Christians. What other instance of this sort do you recall?
    (c) Perhaps the town clerk, like the "chief officers of Asia" (verse 31), favored Paul.

Read the entire account of this riot, verses 23-41, and compel your imagination to picture to you the scenes described by Luke.

Study XVI.—From Ephesus to Corinth

Fifth Day: Paul Goes to Macedonia and Writes Second Corinthians

Shortly after the riot at Ephesus, Paul left for Macedonia. He had previously instructed Titus, who had gone to Corinth, to meet him at Troas. Not finding Titus at Troas, Paul was greatly disappointed, and went on into Macedonia. In Macedonia, Titus came to Paul, bringing news that the Corinthians had punished the offender against whom Paul had written, and that the four factions of the Church had now resolved themselves into two: the followers of Paul and the enemies of Paul. The enemies of Paul attacked his claim to apostleship, accused him of vacillation, and even criticised his speech and personal appearance. Paul then wrote his *Second Epistle to the Corinthians*, which is the most personal of all his letters, since it is filled with allusions to himself, his experiences, his inner life, his thoughts and fears.

1. Paul's departure for Macedonia:
   (a) Read Acts 20:1.
   (b) He fails to find Titus at Troas: 2 Cor. 2:12 and 13.
   (c) Locate Troas.
2. Titus joins Paul in Macedonia: 2 Cor. 7:5-7.
   (a) What kind of news does Titus bring Paul concerning the Church at Corinth?
   (b) Titus is accompanied by two unknown brethren: 2 Cor. 8:18 and 8:22-24.

PRAYER: "O God, since Thou art love, and he that loveth not Thee and his brethren knoweth Thee not, and abideth in death, deliver us from injustice, envy, hatred, and malice; give us grace to pardon all who have offended us, and to bear with one another, even as Thou, Lord, dost bear with us, in Thy patience and great, loving kindness." *Amen.*

Study XVI.—From Ephesus to Corinth
Sixth Day: Second Corinthians (Continued)

Second Corinthians is very difficult to study owing to the uncertainty of the order of the events to which it refers, and owing to the obscurity of many of its allusions. On the other hand, the letter is unusually rich in autobiographical material. Some of this material has already been used for study: such as Paul's illness at Ephesus, his troubles, his anxious suspense while waiting for Titus to return from Corinth, his joy at learning of the obedience of the Corinthian Church. The verses yet remaining for study are chiefly those relating to Paul's defense of himself against his enemies.

1. Paul had earlier changed his original plan of visiting Corinth, whereupon his enemies accused him of weakness and vacillation: 2 Cor. 1:15-24.
2. Some of the insinuations of Paul's enemies: 2 Cor. 10:10.
3. In defending himself against those who attacked his claim to apostleship, Paul proudly reviews his life among the Corinthians; he denounces his enemies, and boasts of his Hebrew blood: 2 Cor. 11:1-22.
4. Paul tells of his sufferings and labors for the cause of Christ: 2 Cor. 11:23-28. In these verses, Paul mentions many events not given at all by Luke in the book of Acts.
    (a) Verse 23: Only one imprisonment of Paul is known from Luke's narrative. Where did it take place?
    (b) Verse 24: Luke says nothing about these five Jewish scourgings.
    (c) Verse 25: Luke tells of only one occasion when Paul was beaten with rods; where was it? Paul says also he was shipwrecked thre times, and that once he was in the water twenty-four hours. Nothing is known concerning these experiences.
5. From verses 23-27 of chapter 11 of Second Corinthians it is clear that there are many unwritten and unknown chapters in the life of St. Paul. Some of these experiences he may have had during his long stay at Ephesus, while engaged in preaching tours away from the city.
6. Paul's vision of Christ: 2 Cor. 12:1-6. What bearing has this vision of Christ as a defense of Paul's apostleship? See Acts 1:21, and page 21, section 6, of these *Studies*.

Study XVI.—From Ephesus to Corinth
Seventh Day: Paul Arrives at Corinth: He Writes the Epistle to the Romans

After a sojourn in Macedonia, Paul came into Greece. He made Corinth his headquarters, and while in that city wrote his *Epistle to the Romans,* which, of all his letters, is the most systematic. In it he sets forth the doctrine of "Justification by Faith." The letter contains only a very few allusions to the apostle himself.

1. Read Acts 20, verse 1 (latter part), verse 2, and the first clause of verse 3.
2. By "Greece" Luke means Greece proper, or the province of Achaia, of which the capital was Corinth.

THE CHURCH AT ROME

While in Corinth, Paul wrote a letter to the Church at Rome. It is not likely that the Church at Rome was founded by any one of the apostles. It seems to have been composed largely of Gentiles, many of whom were proselytes. Probably Gentile and Jewish Christians from Judea, Syria, Asia Minor, and Greece had settled in Rome, attracted thither on business, and had formed a church in the city.

PAUL'S LETTER TO THE ROMANS

Paul had now preached the Gospel from Judea around through Asia Minor as far as the west coast of Greece; he now plans to go to Italy and Spain. But first he must carry the collection for the poor to Jerusalem. Evidently he fears that the Judaizing teachers who had tampered with the Galatians and the Corinthians might go to Rome before he should return from Jerusalem. He therefore writes to prepare the Roman Christians against these false teachers, and also to give them such advice as they, being Gentiles, would especially need.

    (a) Paul has preached the Gospel fully in the East, and now plans to visit Rome and Spain: Romans 15:18-24.
    (b) He must first go to Jerusalem: Romans 15:25-28.
    (c) He fears trouble at Jerusalem: Romans 15:30-33.

That part of Romans best known and oftenest read is, perhaps, chapter 12. It abounds in practical exhortations to purity of spiritual life and to kindness and love in the dealings of Christians one with another. Read carefully Romans 12. Memorize verse 10, and make it your motto to-day.

Study XVII.—**Paul's Last Journey to Jerusalem**
First Day: Paul Leaves Corinth and Goes to Troas in Asia

After staying three months in Greece, Paul planned to sail to Syria. Learning of this, his enemies sought to kill him, whereupon he changed his plan, and journeyed through Macedonia to Troas in Asia. He was now on his way to Jerusalem, bearing a gift of money for the poor of that city, and accompanied by representatives of the churches which had contributed.

1. Read Acts 20:3-6.
2. Verse 3: Had Paul ever been in danger before from the Jews at Corinth?
3. Why did Paul go to Jerusalem at this time? Rom. 15:24 and 25.
4. The collection for the poor at Jerusalem had long been a project very close to Paul's heart:
    (a) The first mention of the collection: Gal. 2:9 and 10.
    (b) Instructions sent to Galatia and Corinth: 1 Cor. 16:1-5 and 2 Cor. 9:1-4.
5. There were many poor people in the Christian Church at Jerusalem: See Acts 2:44 and 45; 4:34 and 35:
    (a) When did Paul on an earlier occasion carry relief to the sufferers at Jerusalem? Acts 11:27-30.
    (b) The Jerusalem Christians may have been impoverished through persecution: 1 Thess. 2:14.
6. Verse 6: Paul's route lay through Philippi. At Philippi, Luke joined Paul's party, as is clear from the use of "we" in this verse. The last preceding *we*-section of Acts ends in chapter 16, verse 16, where Luke was left behind at Philippi.
7. The men who accompanied Paul seem to have been representatives of the churches which had contributed to the collection for the poor. From Macedonia came Aristarchus and Secundus of Thessalonica, Sopater of Berea, and Luke of Philippi; from Corinth, Paul himself may have been the representative; from Asia came Tychicus and Trophimus; and from Galatia, Gaius of Derbe and Timothy of Lystra.
8. Verse 6: The "days of unleavened bread" were the eight days of the Passover festival. In this year (58 A.D.) the days of unleavened bread extended from March 27th to April 3d.

Study XVII.—Paul's Last Journey to Jerusalem
Second Day: Paul Preaches at Troas

When Paul and his party arrived at Troas, the Christians of that city gathered together to celebrate the Lord's Supper and to listen to instruction in Christian doctrine.

1. Read Acts 20:7-12.
2. What is meant by the words "to break bread"?
3. On this occasion Paul may have repeated the words he wrote to the Corinthians concerning the Lord's Supper: 1 Cor. 11:23-30.
4. Verse 7: The "first day of the week," that is, the day *after* the Jewish Sabbath, soon came to be regarded among the Christians as a day peculiarly appropriate for worship; it was the day of the week on which Christ rose from the grave.
5. Verse 8: What other upper chambers, wherein precious memories centered, are mentioned in the New Testament?
6. Verses 8-12: There were many lights in the chamber, the air was heated, and Eutychus sat in the window for the sake of coolness. Overcome by drowsiness, he fell from the window. Luke, who was a physician, says that he was dead when taken up.
7. By prayer, no doubt, Paul caused the life of Eutychus to be restored. Compare 2 Kings 4:33-35. Eutychus was probably left in the care of Luke while Paul continued his discourse.
8. Verse 11: Paul's address lasted all night. On a later occasion at Rome, he spoke all day: Acts 28:23.
9. Mark Troas with a cross on your outline map.

Prayer: "O my God, by whose loving Providence, sorrows, difficulties, trials, dangers become means of grace, lessons of patience, channels of hope, grant us good will to use and not abuse those our privileges; and, of Thy great goodness, keep us alive through this dying life, that out of death Thou mayest raise us up to immortality. For His sake who is the Life, Jesus Christ our Lord." Amen.

STUDY XVII.—**Paul's Last Journey to Jerusalem**
THIRD DAY: FROM TROAS TO MILETUS

Leaving Troas, Paul went overland to Assos, and thence by ship to Mitylene. From Mitylene he sailed past Chios and Samos, but stopped at Trogyllium. On the following day he arrived at Miletus.

1. Read Acts 20:13-16.
2. The distance overland from Troas to Assos is about twenty miles. An excellent road connected these towns. What reason can you give for the fact that Paul went overland to Assos *alone,* while his companions went around by sea?
3. Trace Paul's course on the map from Troas to Miletus.
4. Verse 15: In the A.V., after the words "we arrived at Samos," the clause "and tarried at Trogyllium" is added. The clause does not appear in the R.V. Trogyllium is a promontory that juts out from the mainland alongside of Samos.
5. Miletus lay about twenty-five miles southward from Ephesus. A city of importance in earlier times, it had declined so that in the days of St. Paul it was of little prominence.
   (a) Had Paul ever preached in Miletus?
   (b) Mark Miletus with a cross upon your outline map.
6. Paul had lived at Ephesus for three years (54 to 57 A.D.). To visit Ephesus would require a great deal of time, owing to the large number of acquaintances he had there. Hence he passed by the city.
7. Verse 16:
   (a) Paul had left Philippi after the Passover: See Acts 20:6, and page 129, section 8, of these *Studies.*
   (b) How long after the Passover was the day of Pentecost? See page 22, section 2.
   (c) What special events did the Christians associate with the Passover and with the day of Pentecost?

Study XVII.—**Paul's Last Journey to Jerusalem**

Fourth Day: Paul's Address to the Elders of Ephesus at Miletus

On this journey to Jerusalem, Paul had the conviction that bonds and afflictions awaited him. Feeling that he should not be able to see the Elders of the Ephesian Church again, he sent for them to come to him at Miletus. When they had arrived, Paul made to them a farewell address.

The first part of this address, which will be studied to-day, is a review of Paul's labors among the Ephesians.

1. Read Acts 20:17-27.
2. Verse 17: Why did Paul not stop at Ephesus, and there deliver this address?
3. Verses 18-21: What success did Paul have in his labors at Ephesus? See Acts 19:10, and 19:26.
4. Verses 22 and 23: There were prophets in the early Christian Church. Some of these warnings may have come from them.
5. Verse 24: "So that I may accomplish my course." Paul often speaks of the Christian life as a race for a prize: See 1 Cor. 9:24, and Philippians 3:13 and 14.
6. Verse 25: Paul's words in this verse should not be taken as an inspired prophecy, but rather as a strong conviction. He probably *did* visit Ephesus again, some years later, and when he came, it is unlikely that he saw more than a few, if any, of the Elders whom he now addresses.
7. Verse 26: For the interpretation of this verse read Ezekiel 33:8.

A Summary of Paul's Work: Paul had now preached the Gospel in four provinces of the Roman Empire—Galatia, Asia, Macedonia, and Greece: "From Jerusalem round about to Illyricum, I have fully preached the Gospel of Christ." He had held his own against the Judaizing Christians within the Church and the unbelieving Jews outside of it. Now he is on his way to Jerusalem, bearing a collection for the poor from the churches of Asia Minor and Europe—the gift of Gentiles to Jews. No wonder that in the face of the dangers before him he can speak of finishing his course "with joy." Read again Acts 20:24.

Study XVII.—Paul's Last Journey to Jerusalem
Fifth Day: Paul's Address at Miletus (Continued)

The second part of Paul's address consists of solemn warnings and exhortations. He bids the Ephesian Elders to beware of factions and heresies, and exhorts them to remember the words of the Lord Jesus.

1. Read Acts 20:28-38.
2. Verses 29-31:
   (a) From Paul's *Epistle to the Ephesians,* written a few years after this occasion, it is clear that certain strange doctrines were introduced in Asia. These doctrines seem to be the result of a blending together of Oriental mysticism, Greek philosophy, and Christianity.
   (b) Read Revelation 2:1-6, remembering that Revelation was written probably between 90 and 100 A.D.
3. Verse 34: "These hands": Paul then held up his hands, worn with the labor of tent-making.
4. Verse 35: The words of Jesus, quoted in this verse, are not found in any one of the four Gospels. A few other sayings also are preserved which, like this, are not included in the Gospels.
5. Verses 36-38: In the simple narrative of these three verses we see how strong were the friendships of St. Paul. He loved the Ephesians, and had completely won their hearts.

The "Words of the Lord Jesus": In verse 35 of to-day's lesson, Paul quotes certain words of Jesus. These words are not found in any of the Gospels. It should be remembered that at this time Luke, the writer of the Gospel which bears his name, was with Paul. Luke had probably already begun to gather the material for his "Life of Christ"; he must often have talked with Paul about the Gospel he was about to write. There are several passages in Paul's letters which are thought to be due to the influence of Luke, or possibly to be quotations from his writings.

Study XVII.—**Paul's Last Journey to Jerusalem**

Sixth Day: From Miletus to Ptolemais

From Miletus, Paul went by sea to Patara, touching at Coos and Rhodes. At Patara he took a ship for Phœnicia. Landing at Tyre, he remained seven days, and then sailed to Ptolemais.

1. Read Acts 21:1-7.
2. Trace Paul's course on the map from Miletus to Ptolemais.
3. Verse 3: Paul at Tyre in Phœnicia.
    (a) Had the Gospel been preached in Phœnicia? See Acts 11:19, and 15:1-3.
    (b) Mark Tyre with a cross on your outline map.
4. Verse 4: Compare with this verse, Acts 20:22 and 23.
5. Verse 5: Paul *may* have visited Tyre eight years before this occasion, when on his way to Jerusalem with Barnabas, to consider the relation of Gentile converts to the Mosaic Law (Study XI, page 81). Now, after a visit of only seven days, the whole Church at Tyre escorts Paul to his ship—a strong proof of the affection which they felt toward him. Compare Acts 20:36-38.
6. Verse 7: Locate Ptolemais on your map, and mark it with a cross.

Thought for the Day: From verse 5 of to-day's lesson it is easy to infer that Paul was a man who had the affection of his friends. What qualities have you learned to admire in him?

Prayer: "Confirm, O Lord, we pray Thee, the hearts of Thy children, and strengthen them with the power of Thy grace; that we may both be devout in prayer to Thee, and sincere in our love for each other; through Jesus Christ our Lord." *Amen.*

Study XVII.—Paul's Last Journey to Jerusalem
Seventh Day: From Ptolemais to Jerusalem: Paul's Imprisonment Prophesied

From Ptolemais, Paul went to Cæsarea, where he remained some days. The Feast of the Pentecost was now about two weeks away. Finally, at the Feast of the Pentecost, Paul went up to Jerusalem.

1. Read Acts 21:8-17.
2. Verse 8: Philip the Evangelist:
   (a) What do you remember concerning Philip?
   (b) Who were "the seven," and why were they appointed?
3. Verse 10: Agabus:
   (a) Has Agabus been mentioned before in Acts? If so, where?
   (b) Agabus delivered his prophecy in a symbolical manner, just as the prophets of Old Testament times used to do.
   (c) This prophecy uttered by Agabus seems to have been the most definite and exact of any that had been made during the trip to Jerusalem. Even the fellow-travelers of Paul now urge him not to go to Jerusalem.
4. Verse 13: Compare with this verse, Acts 20:22-24.
5. Verses 15-17:
   (a) "We took up our baggage," R.V. The A.V. has the quaint phrase, "we took up our carriages."
   (b) Perhaps Mnason was converted as early as the time of the first Christian Pentecost. If not a Greek, he was probably a Greek Jew.

Review of Study XVII.—Read rapidly the introductory paragraphs of the lessons of this Study. What do you consider the most important thing contained in the lessons of this week?

PART VII

Paul's Arrest at Jerusalem and Voyage to Rome

Study XVIII.—Paul's Arrest at Jerusalem
Study XIX.—Paul Appears before Felix, Festus, and Agrippa: He Appeals to Cæsar
Study XX.—Paul is Sent to Rome: His Voyage and Shipwreck

Study XVIII.—**Paul's Arrest at Jerusalem**

First Day: Paul's Conference with the Elders

On the day following his arrival at Jerusalem, Paul had a conference with James and the elders. His first concern was to deliver the collection he had gathered for the poor; he also told his hearers of his successful work among the Gentiles. The elders urged him to observe certain Jewish rites during the Pentecost festival, in order that those Jewish Christians who were zealous for the Law of Moses might not stir up trouble against him.

1. Read Acts 21:17-25.
2. What do you recall, from previous study, concerning James?
3. Where were the other apostles?
4. Verses 18-20: Nothing is said concerning the gratitude of the Jerusalem Church for the collection brought by Paul. It seems, also, as though their zeal for the Law of Moses was greater than their joy at the conversion of the Gentiles.
5. Verses 20 and 21: Very many Jewish Christians had not broken at all with Judaism. They kept all the feasts, and observed all the ceremonies of the Jewish religion, but supplemented them with Christian rites and ceremonies. It was right for them that they should do so. The religion of the Old Testament had prepared the way for that of the New Testament; a violent break with the past would have unsettled many of the Jews, accustomed as they were to the religion of their fathers. Their mistake, however, was in insisting that Gentiles should also observe all the laws of Moses and keep all the religious rites of the Jewish Church.
6. Was Paul guilty of the charge made in verse 21?
7. Verses 23 and 24 refer to the vow of a Nazarite. Had Paul ever kept such a vow? If so, when and where?
8. For the vow of a Nazarite, see Numbers 6:1-21.

In the time of Paul the period of a Nazarite vow seems to have lasted thirty days. At the end of that period the person who had made the vow announced to the priest that he was about to begin his seven days of purification. As may be learned from Numbers 6:1-21, each person had to offer two rams, a sheep, a basket of unleavened cakes, and a libation of wine. On account of the expense, the custom arose of allowing someone to take part in the purification ceremonials and defray the cost of the offerings. This St. Paul was asked to do for the four men mentioned in verse 23.

Study XVIII.—Paul's Arrest at Jerusalem
Second Day: A Mob Attacks Paul

Paul followed the advice of the elders, and undertook the purification ceremonies of a Nazarite. While he was in the temple, certain Jews stirred up a mob, took Paul from the temple, and prepared to kill him. Roman soldiers rescued Paul, and began to take him up into the tower adjoining the temple; they stopped, however, on the stairs to allow Paul to address the mob.

1. Read Acts 21:26-40.
2. Verse 26: Paul was guilty of no inconsistency in taking part in this vow. He was a Jew, and observed very many Jewish rites and ceremonies. He maintained, however, that Gentile Christians *should not be compelled* to adopt and observe all the rules of Judaism.
3. Verse 28: Surrounding the temple was a low stone parapet, with an inscription in Latin and Greek:

    "No stranger is to enter within the balustrade and embankment around the sacred place. Whoever is caught will be answerable for his death which will ensue."

4. Why did they take Paul from the temple?
5. Verse 32: The Roman garrison was in a tower called *Antonia*, adjoining the temple on the northwest side, and communicating with it by means of an outside stairway.
6. Why did Paul address the chief captain—a Roman—in Greek? For the name of the chief captain, see Acts 23:26.
7. Verse 38: This Egyptian impostor had gathered together a multitude of people on the Mount of Olives, promising that at his command the walls of Jerusalem would fall. The Romans drove him away, and slew many of his adherents.

"Born the equal of any subject, Paul was bred where that inheritance was peculiarly significant. It is not strange, therefore, that he alone of the apostles showed at all times a sense of high worldly station. His aristocratic consciousness was ingrained . . . witness the calm dignity of his address to the commander of Antonia; the quiet authority with which he called to account the magistrates of Philippi whom other Jews in that city would have approached as Shylock approached Bassanio; the unembarrassed mien with which he rebuked Agrippa and instructed Festus."—Wright, *Cities of Paul.*

STUDY XVIII.—Paul's Arrest at Jerusalem
THIRD DAY: PAUL'S SPEECH ON THE CASTLE STAIRS

Standing on the stairs of the castle, Paul addressed the mob in the Aramaic tongue, their national language. The men listened to him attentively as he told the story of his life, but when he spoke of his commission to preach to the Gentiles, they began to utter violent and frenzied cries against him.

1. Read Acts 22:1-22.
2. From verse 2 it is clear that the mob expected that Paul would address them in Greek—a language which most, if not all, of them understood. Why did Paul use the Aramaic tongue?
3. This speech of Paul's is most tactful; he uses Aramaic rather than Greek; he seeks to show his knowledge of the law and his great regard for Jewish institutions; he appeals to his hearers along those lines in which they are most interested:
    (a) He is a Jew, a pupil of the most celebrated Rabbi of the time, and had been a zealot for the Law (verses 1-3).
    (b) He persecuted the Christians, and was entrusted by the high priest with the commission of stamping out the Church in other cities (4 and 5).
    (c) His vision of Christ (verses 6-11). His Jewish hearers believed in visions in which God revealed Himself to His people. Their past history was one continuous revelation of God.
4. Was there anything in Paul's address, as far as verse 20, that would offend or irritate his listeners?
5. Why were the Jews so much enraged by the statement contained in verse 21?
6. Verse 21: Compare with this verse, Acts 9:15.

THOUGHT FOR THE DAY: The lesson of to-day shows clearly how strong were the religious prejudices of the Jews, and how easily they could be aroused. Among us, at the present time, there are people who cannot see much that is good in those who do not belong to their own branch or denomination of the Christian Church. What spirit do you maintain toward those who do not believe as you do? May they not be as acceptable to God as you are?

STUDY XVIII.—Paul's Arrest at Jerusalem
FOURTH DAY: PAUL'S ROMAN CITIZENSHIP SAVES HIM FROM SCOURGING

Inasmuch as Paul's speech was delivered in Aramaic, it is unlikely that the chief captain understood what was said. Nor did he know what charges were brought against the apostle. After removing Paul to the castle, the chief captain determined to scourge him—a cruel method of wringing the truth from an accused man. Paul, however, appealed to his rights as a Roman citizen, and so escaped from the scourging.

1. Read Acts 22:23-29.
2. Why did the Jews cast off their clothes (verse 23)? See p. 39, section 4. For the throwing of dust, see 2 Samuel 16:13.
3. "Under the Roman system of scourging, the culprit was stripped and tied in a bending posture to a pillar, or stretched on a frame, and the punishment was inflicted with a scourge made of leathern thongs weighted with sharp pieces of bone or lead."
4. Verse 25:
    (a) The thongs were used in binding Paul fast to the pillar or frame on which he was to be scourged.
    (b) The Porcian Law forbade the scourging of a Roman citizen.
    (c) On what occasion before this, as narrated by Luke, was Paul beaten by Roman officers? For other beatings not mentioned by Luke, see 2 Cor. 11:24 and 25.
5. Verse 28: In the early part of the reign of Claudius (41-54 A.D.) Roman citizenship was sold at a high price.
6. Had Paul ever before appealed to his right as a Roman citizen?

CHRISTIAN CITIZENSHIP: The rights of Roman citizenship meant much to Paul; several times in his writings he makes use of figures of speech derived from the Roman political world: heaven is a commonwealth, Christians are its citizens. "Our citizenship is in heaven; from whence also we wait for a Saviour, the Lord Jesus Christ" (Phil. 3:20). "So then ye are no more strangers and sojourners, but ye are fellow-citizens with the saints" (Eph. 2:19).

Study XVIII.—Paul's Arrest at Jerusalem
Fifth Day: Paul Before the Sanhedrin

The chief captain did not understand at all the questions at issue between the Jews and Paul. He had been unable to scourge Paul, and so had failed to learn anything from the apostle himself. Therefore, on the day following the arrest, the chief captain brought Paul before the Jewish Sanhedrin. After the hearing was over, Paul was taken back to the castle.

1. Read Acts 22:30.
2. The Sanhedrin:
    (a) Who composed the Sanhedrin? See page 29, section 3.
    (b) What were the powers of this body?
    (c) Had Paul had anything to do with the Sanhedrin before this time?
3. Read Acts 23:1-5.
4. Paul's conduct toward the high priest:
    (a) The action of Ananias was illegal: John 7:51.
    (b) Ananias, the high priest (47-59 A.D.), was a man of hot temper, and guilty of rapacity and violence. He took tithes by force, robbed inferior priests of their dues, and even let them die of starvation. He was murdered in 59 A.D.
    (c) From Paul's apology in verse 5 it would seem that he did not really know that the person giving the command was the high priest. For the quotation which Paul gives, see Exodus 22:28.
5. Read Acts 23:6-10:
    (a) Was Paul by training and sympathy a Pharisee or a Sadducee?
    (b) What were the beliefs of the Pharisees and the Sadducees?
    (c) Was Paul's conduct on this occasion defensible? Paul certainly regarded the resurrection as a fundamental doctrine of the Christian religion, but was he "called in question of the hope and resurrection of the dead"? Is he not guilty of introducing a false issue?
    (d) What light do verses 20 and 21 of Acts 24 throw on this point?

Thought for the Day: Paul's conduct on this occasion seems not to have been altogether right. He was a human being, and liable to error and sin. Think what he might have done had he not been converted. When you are tempted to criticise Christians for their shortcomings, stop and think what they would be *without* their religion.

STUDY XVIII.—**Paul's Arrest at Jerusalem**

SIXTH DAY: THE JEWS PLOT TO KILL PAUL

During the night following Paul's hearing before the Sanhedrin the Lord appeared to him in a vision, and bade him be of good cheer. The next day more than forty Jews formed a plot to kill Paul; but the plot was made known to the chief captain by Paul's nephew.

1. Read Acts 23:11-22.
2. Verse 11:
    (a) What other occasions do you recall in which Paul, when in danger, was reassured by a vision?
    (b) Had Paul ever planned to visit Rome? See Acts 19:21 and Romans 1:11-13.
3. Verses 16-19: This is the only reference in the New Testament to Paul's sister. Whether she and her husband were Christians, or not, cannot be known.
    (a) There can have been little secrecy on the part of the conspirators.
    (b) From verse 19 it would seem that the agitation of the young man (or boy) was so great that the chief captain took him by the hand to reassure him. What light does this throw on the character of the chief captain?

PRAYER: "O God, who seest all our weaknesses, and the troubles we labor under, have regard unto the prayers of Thy servant, who stands in need of Thy comfort, Thy direction, and Thy help. Thou alone knowest what is best for me; let me never dispute Thy wisdom or Thy goodness. Lord, so prepare my heart, that no affliction may ever so surprise as to overbear me. Dispose me at all times to a readiness to suffer what Thy Providence shall order or permit. Grant that I may never murmur at Thy appointments, nor be exasperated at the administration of Thy Providence." *Amen.*

Study XVIII.—**Paul's Arrest at Jerusalem**

Seventh Day: Paul Is Sent to Cæsarea

When the chief captain had learned of the plot to kill Paul, he made ready an escort of soldiers, and sent Paul from Jerusalem to Cæsarea. He dispatched, also, a letter to Felix, the Roman procurator of Judea, giving him an outline of Paul's case. When Paul reached Cæsarea, Felix arranged to have a hearing as soon as the apostle's accusers should come.

1. Read Acts 23:23-35.
2. Verse 23: The number of soldiers sent with Paul should be noted carefully. At this time the country was in an unsettled condition; there had been in the recent past uprisings and tumults (see Acts 5:36 and 37, and chapter 21:38); the chief captain may have feared, also, that the Jews would attempt to take Paul away from the soldiers.
3. The letter of the chief captain, verses 26-30, merits careful perusal.
    (a) It was written by a Roman to a Roman, on official business. What language was employed?
    (b) Is verse 27 quite in accordance with the truth?
    (c) What does Claudius Lysias suppress in this letter?
4. Verse 34: Cilicia seems at this time to have been attached for administrative purposes to Syria, hence the willingness of Felix to hear the case.
5. Antonius Felix was appointed procurator by the Emperor Claudius, in 52 A.D. He married a Jewess, Drusilla, the daughter of Agrippa I, after taking her away from her husband, Azizus. "Felix had been a slave, and Tacitus says that he retained the temper of a slave after he had been set free and clothed with great power. He was a man of lust and blood. The only remedy he had for the crimes and disorders of Judea was force."—*Gilbert.*
6. Cæsarea was built by Herod the Great, and was named after the Emperor. Herod's palace was now the official residence of the Roman procurator. Here Paul was kept for two years. It is likely that his quarters were comfortable; after no great time he was given a good deal of liberty, and was allowed to see his friends.

Review Thought: What event in the portion of Paul's life studied this week has seemed to you most significant? Review the opening paragraphs of the lessons of this Study.

STUDY XIX.—Paul Appears Before Felix, Festus, and Agrippa: He Appeals to Cæsar

FIRST DAY: PAUL'S HEARING BEFORE FELIX

Five days after the hearing before the Sanhedrin, the high priest Ananias and the elders came to Cæsarea to accuse Paul. Since they were unused to procedure before a Roman magistrate, they took with them a professional advocate, Tertullus. To-day's lesson contains the speech of Tertullus and Paul's reply.

1. Read Acts 24:1-21.
2. Tertullus was a Roman advocate, or *causidicus,* hired for the occasion. He begins his speech by complimenting Felix.
    (a) What two services does Tertullus say Felix has rendered the Jewish nation?
    (b) Were these statements true? What had been the attitude of Felix toward the Jews? See page 145, section 5.
3. The accusation (verse 5):
    (a) What three charges does Tertullus bring against Paul?
    (b) Were these charges true?
4. Paul's answer to the accusation (verses 10-21):
    (a) How does the opening of Paul's speech (verse 10) compare with that of Tertullus?
    (b) It was now the year 58 A.D. Felix became procurator in 52 A.D.
    (c) Verse 11: The events of the twelve days may be accounted for as follows:

Day		Acts
1	Arrival at Jerusalem	21:17
2	Interview with James	21:18
3-7	Vow and arrest	21:26 and 27
8	Hearing before the Sanhedrin	22:30
9	The conspiracy	23:12
10	Arrival at Cæsarea	23:33
11-12	In custody	23:35
13	The hearing at Cæsarea	24:1

5. How does Paul answer the charges of Tertullus?
6. How do you interpret verses 20 and 21? Did Paul do wrong at the hearing before the Sanhedrin?

MEMORY VERSE: Memorize verse 16 of to-day's lesson.

STUDY XIX.—**Paul Appears Before Felix, Festus, and Agrippa: He Appeals to Cæsar**

SECOND DAY: PAUL'S PRIVATE AUDIENCE WITH FELIX AND DRUSILLA

Impressed by the bearing and words of his prisoner, Felix dismissed the Jews, and put Paul under the care of a centurion; he ordered, also, that the apostle should have liberty to see his friends. Some days later, Paul had a private audience with Felix and Drusilla, in which he spoke with such effect that he greatly moved the guilty conscience of Felix. Yet Paul was kept a prisoner during the time of Felix's governorship. Two years later, Felix was succeeded by Porcius Festus.

1. Read Acts 24:22-27.
2. Verse 10: It was now the year 58 A.D. Felix became procurator in 52 A.D.
3. Verse 22: How did it happen that Felix had a "more exact knowledge concerning the Way"? How long had he been in Palestine? Who was his wife? See verse 24.
4. Verse 23: What do you suppose it was in Paul's manner and bearing that led Felix to give him so much liberty?
5. Verse 24: Why did Felix have Paul come and speak before Drusilla and himself?
6. Verse 25: Why did Felix tremble when Paul reasoned of "righteousness, temperance, and judgment to come"?
7. Verse 26: Why did Felix think that Paul or his friends had money?
8. How do you suppose Paul used his two years at Cæsarea (verse 27)?
9. Verse 27: When Felix was succeeded by Porcius Festus, did he do right in leaving Paul in prison?

THOUGHT FOR THE DAY: "When I have a convenient season, I will call thee unto me." Do you ever use such words as these of Felix, when your conscience has been moved? Are you postponing until a convenient season some step that you ought to take in your Christian life? Are you willing to take that step to-day?

STUDY XIX.—**Paul Appears Before Felix, Festus, and Agrippa: He Appeals to Cæsar**

THIRD DAY: PAUL'S HEARING BEFORE FESTUS

As soon as the new procurator, Festus, had taken up the duties of his office, the high priest and elders reopened the case against St. Paul. A hearing was held at Cæsarea. Festus, in order to please the Jews, attempted to transfer the case to the Jewish Council, whereupon Paul appealed to Cæsar. This appeal took the matter entirely out of the hands of Festus.

1. Read Acts 25:1-12.
2. Why did Festus go to Jerusalem?
3. What reason had the Jews to think that Festus would grant the request of verses 2 and 3?
4. This request came from the most important men in Jerusalem. It is to the credit of Festus that he refused to do as they wished; he may have known that they were planning to kill Paul.
5. Judging from verse 8, what charges were brought against Paul? Compare this verse with Acts 24:12. What new charge do Paul's accusers put forward?
6. Verse 9: The charges brought against Paul could not be proved; therefore, Paul should have been released. But Felix had been impressed with the vehemence of Paul's accusers (see verse 7), and was not unmindful of the fact that they were the chief men of Jerusalem; hence he proposed that which he had previously refused—to send Paul to Jerusalem.
7. Verses 10 and 11: Paul had the right, as a Roman citizen, to claim exemption from the jurisdiction of the Jewish Sanhedrin. The Roman procurator had just attempted to throw Paul's case back into the hands of the Sanhedrin, hence Paul's appeal to Cæsar.
8. Proconsuls, propraetors, and procurators administered justice in the Roman provinces. A Roman citizen might appeal from their decision to Cæsar.
9. Which one of the Roman Emperors ruled at this time (60 A.D.), and what was his character?

PAUL'S RESPECT FOR AUTHORITY: Read Titus 3:1 and 1 Timothy 2:1 and 2.

Study XIX.—**Paul Appears Before Felix, Festus, and Agrippa: He Appeals to Cæsar**

Fourth Day: Paul Appears Before Agrippa

After Paul had appealed to Cæsar, he remained in prison at Cæsarea, waiting to be sent to Rome. Meanwhile, Agrippa, King of Galilee and the region east of the Jordan, came to pay an official visit to Festus. During the course of this visit Paul was brought before Agrippa for an informal hearing.

1. Read Acts 25:13-27.
2. Agrippa, known accurately as Agrippa II, was the great-grandson of Herod the Great. He was the last of the Herod family celebrated in history. Bernice was his sister.
3. Josephus, the Jewish historian, records the fact that Agrippa displayed great anxiety to stand well with Roman governors. Festus had just entered upon his office, consequently Agrippa came to pay his first official visit.
4. Verses 14-21: Festus detailed Paul's case to Agrippa, hoping that he would be able to suggest what charges should be sent to the Emperor.
5. Verse 23: "The Herods were fond of show, and Festus gratified their humor by a grand processional display. He would doubtless appear in his scarlet *paludament,* with his full attendance of lictors and bodyguards, who would stand at arms behind the gilded chairs which were placed for himself and his distinguished visitors. We are expressly told that Agrippa and Bernice went in state to the Prætorium, she, doubtless, blazing in all her jewels, and he in his purple robes, and both with the golden circlets of royalty around their foreheads, and attended by a suite of followers in the most gorgeous apparel of Eastern pomp."—*Canon Farrar.*
6. Verse 26: Why was Festus anxious to have Agrippa listen to Paul? See Acts 26:2 and 3.
7. Verses 26 and 27: The governor had to send to the Emperor, along with the accused man, an *elogium,* or statement of the crime. It is to this *elogium* that Festus refers in these verses.
8. This hearing before Agrippa was not a judicial trial; the case was no longer under the jurisdiction of Festus—it belonged to the Emperor.

STUDY XIX.—**Paul Appears Before Felix, Festus, and Agrippa: He Appeals to Cæsar**

FIFTH DAY: PAUL'S SPEECH BEFORE AGRIPPA

At the informal hearing before Agrippa, Paul delivered a speech in which he gave an account of his life and labors. This speech may be divided into two parts. The first part, which contains in brief the story of his life until his conversion, will be the subject of to-day's lesson.

1. Read Acts 26:1-11.
2. What promise of the Lord was fulfilled by Paul's appearance before Agrippa? See Acts 9:13-15.
3. Verses 2 and 3: Observe how tactfully Paul begins his speech. Compare with this, Acts 24:10.
4. In verses 6-8, Paul says that the Jews accused him for teaching that Jesus was the Messiah, and that He rose from the dead. Yet the charges of the Jews, as given in Acts 25:8, are that he taught against the Law of Moses, that he profaned the temple, and that he stirred up opposition to Cæsar. Paul is now speaking of the *underlying reason* for the hostility of the Jews.
5. Verse 10: The R.V. reads, "I gave my vote against them." To what body did Paul belong before his conversion, if he had the power of voting against those who were heretics from the Jewish point of view?
6. Verse 11: What verses can you cite to show how Paul persecuted the Christians "even unto foreign cities"?
7. How did Paul's persecution of the Christians directly help the spread of the Gospel?

PRAYER: "We humbly beseech Thee, O heavenly Father, to do away as the night all our transgressions, and to scatter our sins as the morning cloud. Lord, forgive whatsoever is amiss in us, cleanse us from our sin, and let Thy Holy Spirit so go before and accompany and follow us day by day, that we may believe in Thee, and love Thee, and keep Thy commandments, through Jesus Christ our Lord." *Amen.*

Study XIX.—**Paul Appears Before Felix, Festus, and Agrippa: He Appeals to Cæsar**

Sixth Day: Paul's Speech Before Agrippa (Continued)

In the second part of his speech, Paul tells of his conversion and of his activity as a Christian preacher.

1. Read Acts 26:12-23.
2. Verses 12 to 18 contain an account of Paul's conversion. You have already studied two accounts of this event. Where may they be found?
3. Verse 14: This verse contains two statements not found in the preceding accounts of Paul's conversion: that Jesus spoke to Paul in Hebrew (Aramaic), and that He said, "It is hard for thee to kick against the goad" (R.V.).
4. From this use of the figure of an ox kicking against the goad, what do you infer concerning Paul's inward condition just before his conversion?
5. This is the first appearance of Jesus to Paul (verse 15). For other appearances, see Acts 18:9; 22:17 and 18; 2 Cor. 12:1-4; and Acts 23:11. How did these visions enable Paul to answer the charge of his enemies that he was not a true apostle?
6. Verse 20: In what Gentile lands had Paul preached?
7. Who are meant by "the people" of verse 23?

Thought for To-day: Have you ever discovered the truth of the statement that "it is hard to kick against the pricks"? Are you, at the present time, resisting God's will, or refusing to do some duty that you ought to perform?

Prayer: "O Lord, give me grace, by constant obedience to offer up my will and my heart as an acceptable sacrifice unto Thee." Amen.

Study XIX.—**Paul Appears Before Felix, Festus, and Agrippa: He Appeals to Cæsar**

SEVENTH DAY: PAUL'S SPEECH BEFORE AGRIPPA (CONCLUDED)

Much that Paul said was unintelligible to Festus, who finally interrupted him by saying that his mind was unbalanced. Paul then turned to King Agrippa and appealed to him as to the truth of his statements. Agrippa answered Paul with a flippant reply, whereupon the hearing terminated.

1. Read Acts 26:24-32.
2. Remembering that Festus was a Roman, recently come to Palestine, what parts of Paul's speech do you think he would fail to understand?
3. The word translated "learning" (verse 24) is the same word which is rendered "letters" in John 7:14-16. Festus evidently regards Paul as a religious fanatic, crazed by poring over the Scriptures.
4. In verse 26, what does Paul mean by saying, "this hath not been done in a corner"? See John 12:19 and Acts 17:6.
5. The words of Agrippa in verse 28 have generally been misinterpreted and misunderstood; this is due to the fact that they are incorrectly translated in the A.V. The A.V. reads, "Almost thou persuadest me to be a Christian." The R.V. is nearer the original Greek: "With but little persuasion thou wouldst fain make me a Christian." Paul had just said, in verses 22 and 23, that the death and resurrection of Christ were foretold by the prophets. Turning then to Agrippa, he asked: "King Agrippa, believest thou the prophets? I know that thou believest." The inference is, of course, that if Agrippa believed the prophets, he ought also to believe that Jesus was the Messiah promised by them. This inference Agrippa dismissed with the half-jesting, if not contemptuous, reply: "You are trying with little trouble, and in a short time, to make me a Christian."
6. Observe the serious turn which Paul gives to the words of Agrippa as he replies: "I would to God, that whether with little or with much, not thou only, but also all that hear me this day, might become such as I am, except these bonds." (R.V.)

THE NAME CHRISTIAN: What was the origin of the name Christian? What does James say of this name? See James 2:7.

STUDY XX.—**Paul is Sent to Rome: His Voyage and Shipwreck**

FIRST DAY: FROM CÆSAREA TO FAIR HAVENS IN CRETE

When it was decided to send Paul to Rome, he and other prisoners were put on board a vessel that left Cæsarea late in the summer or early in the autumn of 60 A.D. Owing to adverse winds, the sailors were obliged to alter their course and run for safety into a harbor on the south side of Crete.

1. Read Acts 27:1-8.
2. Why was Paul sent to Rome?
3. The merchant ships of the ancients were different from modern sailing vessels in several important respects. Prow and stern were practically alike; there was one mast, carrying a huge, square sail; and there were two paddle-like rudders, which were not hinged like those of modern ships, but were loose, and could be lifted out of the water and lashed fast. The single mast, with its large sail, concentrated upon the hull a great strain whenever there was a strong wind, hence when a storm arose there was danger that the timbers would part. At such times, undergirders were used—cables which were passed around the hull to hold the planks together.
4. What indication do you find in these verses that Luke was with Paul?
5. Locate Adramyttium. What previous mention has been made of Aristarchus? Acts 19:29 and 20:4.
6. Sidon lay on the road between Jerusalem and Antioch, 67 miles from Cæsarea. Had Paul ever been in Sidon?
7. What led Julius to treat Paul with so much consideration (verse 3)? Why did Paul need to "refresh himself" or "receive attention" (R.V. margin) at Sidon?
8. A vessel sailing from Sidon to Adramyttium would naturally pass to the west of Cyprus (see map). But the wind blew from the west or northwest, so that Paul's ship sailed under the lee—that is, to the east of Cyprus—and then took advantage of the current and the land breezes of Cilicia and Pamphylia to reach Myra. Locate Myra.
9. Verses 6 and 7: The strong west or northwest wind still continued to blow. The ship of Alexandria had probably been forced from its course by it. On account of this same wind the ship now has difficulty in going from Myra to Cnidos, and is obliged to run to the southwest, under the lee of Crete, into Fair Havens.

Study XX.—Paul is Sent to Rome: His Voyage and Shipwreck

Second Day: Departure from Crete: A Storm Arises

After the delay in Crete, the season had come in which navigation was dangerous. As Fair Havens was an unsuitable harbor in which to winter, an attempt was made to reach Phœnix, in southwestern Crete, but a violent northeast wind drove them away from the island, off toward the southwest.

1. Read Acts 27:9-19.
2. Verse 9: The Fast was the Jewish Day of Atonement, which was observed about the first of October. In ancient times the period favorable to navigation in the Mediterranean extended from March to October. From October until spring the sky was obscured much of the time, so that the stars could not be observed. It should be remembered that there were no compasses, quadrants, or sextants in those days.
3. What perils had Paul already experienced upon the sea? See 2 Cor. 11:25.
4. Verse 12: Phœnix (or Phenice) was about forty miles west of Fair Havens. The R.V. gives the proper translation of the original—"a haven of Crete looking northeast and southeast," or freely, "a haven looking down along the southwest wind (*Lips*) and the northwest wind (*Choros*)."
5. Verses 13 and 14: The south wind was *Notus*; *Euraquilo* (verse 14) was the northeast wind. The wind suddenly shifted from the south to the northeast, and became what Luke calls a "typhonic wind," for such is the meaning of the word rendered in the R.V. as "tempestuous."
6. Verse 15: The ship was driven to the southwest under Cauda (A.V., Clauda). Cauda is twenty miles from Cape Matala, off Crete.
7. Verse 16: The ship's boat had been towed behind until now.
8. Verse 17: Why did the sailors undergird the ship? The Syrtis (*quicksands*, A.V.) is the Syrtis Major of Africa, off to the southwest, filled with sandbars and shoals.
9. Verses 17-19: The R.V. gives the best translation: "They lowered the gear, and so were driven. And as we labored exceedingly with the storm, the next day they began to throw the freight overboard; and the third day they cast out with their own hands the tackling [furniture] of the ship."

A Storm at Sea: Read verses 23 to 31 of the 107th Psalm.

STUDY XX.—**Paul is Sent to Rome: His Voyage and Shipwreck**

THIRD DAY: THE STORM CONTINUES: PAUL'S VISION: THEY NEAR LAND

The violence of the storm still continued. After some days Paul had a vision in which he was assured that the lives of none on board should be lost. At the end of the second week, the vessel neared land about midnight. The sailors cast out four anchors, and waited for day.

1. Read Acts 27:20-32.
2. Why was the absence of sun and stars a serious misfortune (verse 20)? Why had they been a long time without food (verse 21)?
3. Paul's vision:
   (a) Compare verse 22 with verse 10. Does Paul make the statement in verse 10 by inspiration or on his own authority and judgment?
   (b) Beginning with the first chapter of Acts, what part do angels play in the history of the Christian Church? See Acts 5:19; 8:26; 10:3; 12:7-10.
   (c) Verse 24: How do you interpret the words, "God hath granted thee all them that sail with thee"?
4. The approach to land:
   (a) The Sea of Adria: That part of the Mediterranean between Crete and Sicily was sometimes loosely designated as "the Sea of Adria."
   (b) Why did the sailors surmise that land was near?
5. Verses 30-32: Paul was not heeded when he gave the advice contained in verse 10. Why do the centurion and soldiers obey him so readily now?

PAUL AS A LEADER: "A ship is a kind of miniature of the world. It is a floating island, in which there are the government and the governed. But the government is like that of states, liable to sudden social upheavals, in which the ablest man is thrown to the top. This was a voyage of extreme perils, which required the utmost presence of mind and power of winning the confidence and obedience of those on board. Before it was ended Paul was virtually both the captain of the ship and the general of the soldiers; and all on board owed him their lives."—*Stalker*.

STUDY XX.—**Paul is Sent to Rome: His Voyage and Shipwreck**

FOURTH DAY: THE SHIP GOES TO PIECES: ALL THE MEN REACH LAND

In the morning the sailors raised the anchors, and attempted to run the ship ashore. The ship grounded where two currents met, and was quickly battered to pieces by the waves. The men, on bits of wreckage and by swimming, reached the land.

1. Read Acts 27:33-44.
2. Verse 35: "In the sight of the heathen soldiers and sailors, Paul broke the bread in solemn thanksgiving, and thus converted the whole into a religious act, which can hardly have been without its influence on the minds of some, at all events, of those who had heard St. Paul's previous words about the revelation which God had made to him."—*Lumby*.
3. Verse 36: Paul's reassuring manner and words of good cheer were contagious: the men caught his hopeful spirit.
4. Why did they lighten the ship still further (verse 38)?
5. St. Paul's Bay, in Malta, is pointed out as the scene of Paul's landing. Close inshore is a small island called Salmonetta. Between this island and the shore is a strong current that has formed a mudbank. Here the ship grounded at a point where the current met the waves of the sea. The ship was still a short distance from the land, hence the men had to swim.
6. Verse 42: A Roman soldier might forfeit his own life, if he lost a prisoner.
7. Verse 43: What favors had the centurion already granted Paul? Why did he grant them?

"The calm, the breeze, the gale, the storm,
  The ocean and the land,
All, all are Thine, and held within
  The hollow of Thy hand.

"Across this troubled tide of life
  Thyself our pilot be,
Until we reach that better land,
  The land that knows no sea."

—*Edward A. Dayman.*

Study XX.—**Paul is Sent to Rome: His Voyage and Shipwreck**

FIFTH DAY: THE LANDING ON MALTA: PAUL BITTEN BY A VIPER

When the men from the wrecked vessel had reached land, they found it to be the island of Melita (the modern Malta). While gathering wood for a fire, Paul was bitten by a viper. The natives were surprised that he suffered no harm therefrom, and concluded that he was a god.

1. Read Acts 28:1-6.
2. Verse 1: Melita of this narrative is now generally believed to be Malta, an island 17¼ miles long by 9¼ miles wide, about 60 miles south of Sicily. It was a Roman possession, with the rights of a *municipium,* and belonged to the province of Sicily.
3. Verse 2:
   (a) "The barbarians": The word *barbarians* (Greek $\beta\acute{\alpha}\rho\beta\alpha\rho\text{o}\iota$) was used by the Greeks as the designation of all those who did not speak Greek and were destitute of Greek culture. Judging from the presence of the word in this verse, Luke, the writer of Acts, must have been a Greek. It should also be remembered that he was a physician and a man of no little education.
   (b) The men of Melita were descendants of a Phœnician colony; perhaps they had come from Carthage.
4. Verse 3: Observe that Paul helps the barbarians gather firewood; Paul, wherever he might be, was always energetically and actively engaged in helping others.
5. Verse 4:
   (a) The fact that there are now no vipers in Malta does not prove that there were none eighteen hundred years ago.
   (b) The barbarians knew that Paul was a prisoner, and so thought that he was surely a criminal.
6. Verse 5: Of what promise of Jesus is this verse a fulfilment? See Mark 16:17 and 18. Paul may have had this saying of Jesus in mind; possibly also the promise of Acts 27:24.
7. When and where before this occasion was Paul regarded as a god?

Study XX.—Paul is Sent to Rome: His Voyage and Shipwreck

Sixth Day: Paul Works Miracles in Malta

During the winter season of three months which the shipwrecked men spent in Malta, Paul wrought many miracles. Consequently, when Paul was about to leave the island, the natives gave him and his companions many gifts.

1. Read Acts 28:7-10.
2. The Greek word translated "the chief man," in verse 7, seems to have been an official title. An inscription has been found in Malta in which a certain Roman is designated in the same way. Publius may have been the governor of Malta, serving as deputy to the prætor of Sicily.
3. Verse 7: What other instances of this sort do you recall in which men of wealth or official position were kind to Paul? What was it about Paul that led them to treat him with so much favor?
4. During the three months of his stay in Malta is it likely that Paul did anything else besides heal the sick?
5. Mark Malta with a cross upon your outline map.
6. Tradition asserts that Publius was the first bishop of Malta.
7. Verse 10: Special marks of honor and esteem were given to Paul and his friends. When the whole party of men left the island, all of the soldiers and sailors profited from their association with Paul, Luke, and Aristarchus.

Lesson Thought: Paul began to serve others as soon as he landed on the island of Malta, and he continued to do good throughout his stay. Malta, compared with Macedonia, Greece, or Asia, was a humble field in which to labor, yet the apostle found plenty to do. Do you try to be useful in helping others even when you are among the lowly, and when you are in the unattractive and least inviting places?

Study XX.—Paul is Sent to Rome: His Voyage and Shipwreck

Seventh Day: From Malta to Rome

The centurion and his prisoners remained in Malta three months. Now that the season for navigation was open, they sailed to Italy, landed at Puteoli, and went overland to Rome. At Rome, Paul was allowed to have a lodging by himself, though chained constantly to a Roman soldier.

1. Read Acts 28:11-16.
2. Verse 11: It was now early spring, in the year 61 A.D., and the ship of Alexandria resumed its course to Italy. Its figureheads were images of the Twin Brothers, Castor and Pollux, who, in ancient mythology, were the sons of Zeus and Leda. They were thought to favor sailors in their voyages. Castor and Pollux were identified with the constellation called *Gemini*—one of the signs of the zodiac.
3. Verse 12: Undoubtedly there were Jews at Syracuse. Tradition says that Paul founded a church there. Mark Syracuse with a cross.
4. Verse 13: Locate Rhegium and Puteoli. Puteoli, in the Bay of Naples, was one of the great ports of Rome. Near by were many of the fashionable watering-places of Rome. In plain view, also, was Vesuvius, which a few years later (79 A.D.) broke forth and consumed Pompeii and Herculaneum.
5. Apparently the party did tarry seven days at Puteoli (verse 14). How do you account for the presence of Christian brethren at Puteoli?
6. Meanwhile news had reached Rome that Paul was coming.
    (a) What communication had Paul previously had with the Roman Christians?
    (b) Note that in the sixteenth chapter of Romans, Paul sends personal greetings to no less than twenty-seven members of the Church at Rome. Many of these may have been earlier converts of his in the East.
7. Locate the Market of Appius and the Three Taverns. The former is 40 miles from Rome, the latter 30. The devotion of the men who came as far as these places to meet him greatly cheered Paul.
8. Verse 16: Julius, the centurion, was probably the one who secured this concession for Paul. How long had Julius known Paul? Paul often alludes to his "bonds," meaning the chain by which he was bound to the soldiers who guarded him.

PART VIII

PAUL'S IMPRISONMENT AND DEATH AT ROME

STUDY XXI.—Two Years in Prison at Rome
STUDY XXII.—Paul's Last Travels, Second Imprisonment, and Death

STUDY XXI.—**Two Years in Prison at Rome**

FIRST DAY: PAUL CALLS TOGETHER THE CHIEF JEWS OF ROME

Three days after his arrival at Rome, Paul called together the chief officers of the Jewish synagogues of the city. He did this that he might, by a conference with them, both clear himself of unjust suspicion, and also assure them that he was not seeking to involve the Jews in trouble with the Romans.

1. Read Acts 28:17-22.
2. Verse 17:
    (a) How would Paul naturally spend these first three days?
    (b) How had the Christian Church at Rome come into existence? See page 128.
    (c) Were these chief men of the Jews Christians? See verses 21 and 22.
    (d) Many Jews had been carried to Rome as slaves by Pompey. Most of them were freed at a later time, and some of them even became Roman citizens. They were a wealthy and important class in the population of the city; they had seven synagogues; and they occupied a quarter on the west bank of the Tiber.
3. Verses 17-20: "St. Paul shows himself the patriotic Jew. He knew how many things his fellow-countrymen had suffered at the hands of the Roman power, and he did not wish in any way to bring on them more trouble. He therefore explains that he had taken the course of appealing to Cæsar only because he saw no other means of obtaining his release. If that were secured he wished to lay no charge at the door of his accusers or their brethren in Rome."—*Lumby*.
4. What information does verse 22 give concerning the spread and influence of the Christian Church?
5. The Jews at Rome did not appear at all hostile to Paul, nor did they seem anxious to prosecute him. It was only a few years after the repeal of the edict of Claudius banishing the Jews from Rome; probably they were loath to become again involved in religious controversies and tumults.

Study XXI.—Two Years in Prison at Rome
Second Day: Paul Preaches to the Chief Jews of Rome

In their first interview with Paul the chief Jews of Rome desired him to explain the beliefs of the Christians. Accordingly, on an appointed day they assembled in the house in which Paul was staying. All day long Paul preached to them concerning the Kingdom of God.

1. Read Acts 28:23-29.
2. Verse 23:
    (a) The R.V. has "in great number"; better still, it might be rendered, "they came to him into his lodging *in greater numbers*" (than before).
    (b) Paul was probably lodging in the house of a Christian. Some think it may have been the home of Aquila and Priscilla.
    (c) "From morning till evening." On what occasion did Paul preach all night? See Acts 20:7-11.
3. Verses 25-27: Verify this quotation, which may be found in the sixth chapter of Isaiah.
4. Verse 28 contains the last words of St. Paul which Luke records. It is significant that they were spoken concerning the publishing of the Gospel to the Gentiles. It had been Paul's practice to preach to the Jews first and then to the Gentiles; his work at Rome opens in the same way. See also Romans 1:16.
5. Verse 29: This verse, which is not found in the R.V., is given in the A.V. as follows: "And when he had said these words, the Jews departed, and had great reasoning among themselves." Some of the ancient manuscripts contain the verse, others do not. The best manuscripts agree in omitting it.

Lesson Thought: The despised Gentiles (the Greeks and Romans) were more willing to accept the Gospel than were the proud and exclusive Jews. Are some of your acquaintances, on whom you may look with condescension, if not with contempt, more willing to receive and live the Gospel than you are? Does such pride and self-will become you?

Study XXI.—**Two Years in Prison at Rome**
Third Day: Paul's Manner of Life at Rome

During his imprisonment at Rome, Paul was treated with great consideration; though chained constantly to a Roman soldier, he was allowed to live in his own hired house and receive his friends and any other men who might wish to visit him. He also preached the Kingdom of God with all boldness. At this time, too, he wrote several epistles, which are preserved.

1. Read Acts 28:30 and 31.
2. Verse 30: Where did Paul get the money with which to hire a house? In the epistles of this period he says nothing about working at his trade: in fact, it is unlikely that he did so labor while chained to a Roman soldier. Money, too, would be required to carry his appeal up to Cæsar: there would be lawyers' fees and other expenses. Possibly Paul may have inherited property from his father at this time, or may have had rich and powerful friends who provided for him. Paul always moved and acted like a man accustomed to high social position. He appeared on terms of equality with Roman governors, prætors, and centurions, and was unabashed in the presence of King Agrippa.
3. Paul was a prisoner at Rome during the years 61-63 A.D. Who was the Roman Emperor at that time, and what was his character?
4. Paul was chained constantly to a soldier of the Prætorian guard. These guards relieved one another at intervals. Many a rough soldier would hear Paul as he preached and taught the Gospel, and would then go back to the barracks and repeat what he had heard. Some of these men were converted: see Philippians 1:12 and 13 (R.V.); the word "palace" (A.V.) should be "Prætorium" or "Prætorian guard."
5. Paul's case was delayed for two years. Such delays were inevitable; much would depend on a mere whim of the Emperor; his officers, too, doubtless hoped to get presents of money before introducing the appeal.

Lesson Thought: "Preaching . . . with all boldness, none forbidding him." Truly an astonishing outcome for a prisoner of the Gospel. What English writer, likewise a prisoner because of his religion, wrote a book that has influenced and helped millions of people?

Study XXI.—Two Years in Prison at Rome

Fourth Day: The Epistle to the Philippians

Luke's account of Paul's life and work ends with the verses studied yesterday. The remaining events of his life can be learned only from certain statements concerning himself which he makes in his epistles. During his imprisonment he wrote four epistles that are preserved. The first of these is his *Epistle to the Philippians*.

1. When did Paul first visit Philippi? What were some of the incidents of the visit? How many times did he visit Philippi subsequently?
2. The Church at Philippi had always been dear to Paul's heart. They had sent him gifts of money while he was at Thessalonica on his second missionary journey. During Paul's imprisonment, the Philippians sent Epaphroditus to him with a present. While in Rome, Epaphroditus was ill. When able to return to Philippi, he carried with him *The Epistle to the Philippians*.

THE EPISTLE TO THE PHILIPPIANS

3. Paul's Affection for the Philippians:
    (a) He longs to see them: Phil. 1:7 and 8.
    (b) His gratitude for their kindness to him: Phil. 4:10-18.
4. Glimpses of Paul:
    (a) His influence felt throughout the Prætorian guard: Phil. 1:12-14. Also in Cæsar's household: Phil. 4:22.
    (b) Some Jewish Christians are trying to injure him: Phil. 1:16-19.
    (c) Weary of imprisonment, he sometimes longs to die and be with Christ: Phil. 1:21-24.
    (d) He plans to send Timothy to Philippi: Phil. 2:19-23.
    (e) Paul hopes to visit the Philippians soon himself: Phil. 2:24. He sends Epaphroditus: 2:25, 28 and 29.

A Summary: Read Paul's review of his own career and estimate of his spiritual condition: Philippians 3:4-14.

Study XXI.—Two Years in Prison at Rome
Fifth Day: The Epistle to the Colossians

The second of the four letters, written while Paul was a prisoner at Rome, was *The Epistle to the Colossians*. This letter seems to have been called forth by the appearance of errors in the Church, due to the teaching of certain Jews, and to the introduction of false philosophical doctrines which tended to rob Christ of His position as the Head of the Church and the Saviour of men.

1. Colossæ was a city of Phrygia, on the Lycus River, twenty miles from the Mæander. Locate Colossæ, and mark it on your outline map with a cross.
2. Was Paul ever in Colossæ? See Colossians 2:1.
3. For possible founders of the Colossian Church, see Col. 1:7; 4:12; and 4:17.

THE EPISTLE TO THE COLOSSIANS

4. Paul's Relation to the Church:
   (a) His affection for them: Col. 1:3 and 4.
   (b) He has learned about them from Epaphras: Col. 1:7 and 8.
5. Doctrinal Part:
   (a) Solemn warning against the danger of false philosophy and Jewish teaching: Col. 2:8-23.
6. Hortatory Part:
   (a) Practical advice for Christian living: Col. 3:12-17.
7. Salutations and Personal Matters:
   (a) Tychicus probably bore the letter to Colossæ: Col. 4:7 and 8.
   (b) Who were with Paul at this time? Col. 4:10-14 and 1:1.
   (c) What other letter, now lost, was probably sent at this time? See Col. 4:16.
   (d) Paul's salutation. Read Col. 4:18. Why does Paul add this autograph salutation? See page 108, section 4.

Memory Verse: Memorize Colossians 3:17.

Study XXI.—Two Years in Prison at Rome
Sixth Day: The Epistle to Philemon

When Tychicus carried to Colossæ *The Epistle to the Colossians*, he was accompanied by Onesimus. Onesimus was a runaway slave belonging to Philemon of Colossæ. When Onesimus ran away from Colossæ he came to Rome, and there fell under the influence of Paul and was converted. To restore this slave to the favor of his master, Paul wrote his *Epistle to Philemon*. It is the briefest of Paul's letters; it contains no doctrinal matter, but is simply a letter from one Christian gentleman to another on a subject requiring no little tact.

1. Tychicus and Onesimus left Rome together for Colossæ. In the Epistle to the Colossians, Paul specially commends Onesimus. The letter would, of course, be read publicly in the church, and all the Colossians would know of the change in the character of Onesimus. See Col. 4:7-9 and 4:16.
2. Read the entire *Epistle to Philemon*.
3. Verse 2: Apphia was possibly the wife of Philemon. Archippus was evidently a member of the family, perhaps the son or brother of Philemon. See also Col. 4:17.
4. Verses 8-14: Observe with what tact Paul asks this favor of Philemon.
5. Verse 9: "Paul the aged." How old was Paul at this time? See page 10.
6. Verses 10 and 11: The name *Onesimus* means "profitable." Paul puns on his name; the verses might be rendered: "I beseech thee for my child, whom I have begotten in my bonds, Profitable, who was aforetime Unprofitable to thee, but now *profitable* to thee and to me."
7. What light do verses 19 and 22 throw on Paul's fortunes at this time? See also page 165, section 2.
8. Paul now expects liberation: See verse 22.
9. Observe that those who send greetings, verses 23 and 24, are the same (with one exception) as those who send greetings at the close of *The Epistle to the Colossians*.

"*The Epistle to Philemon* has been described as the letter of a Christian gentleman, animated by strong Christian feeling, tempered with discretion, and expressed with dignity and moderation not untouched with humour."—*McClymont.*

STUDY XXI.—Two Years in Prison at Rome
SEVENTH DAY: THE EPISTLE TO THE EPHESIANS

The Epistle to the Ephesians was probably a general epistle sent to a number of churches in Asia Minor. Three of the best manuscripts of the New Testament do not have the words "at Ephesus" in chapter 1, verse 1. This, coupled with the fact that the letter has no personal references and greetings, has led to the belief given above. When copies of this letter were made for the individual churches, the name of the church was inserted in chapter 1, verse 1.

1. *The Epistle to the Ephesians* was written at the same time as *Colossians* and *Philemon*. In Col. 4:7-9 Paul says he is sending Tychicus to Colossæ; in Ephesians 6:21 and 22, he says he is sending Tychicus to Ephesus (or Asia). Compare especially Col. 4:9 and Eph. 6:22.
2. Tychicus seems to have been the bearer of this epistle as well as *The Epistle to the Colossians*. Onesimus probably carried *The Epistle to Philemon*.

THE EPISTLE TO THE EPHESIANS

"It has been said by Coleridge that this is one of the divinest compositions of man. It embraces every doctrine of Christianity; first, those doctrines peculiar to Christianity; secondly, those precepts common to it with natural religion. . . . The first half of the Epistle is, for the most part, a hymn of praise for the *grace of God*, manifested according to His good pleasure which He purposed in Himself—accompanied with the apostle's prayer for his readers that they may realize the glory of their *calling*. . . . In the second part the apostle descends by a swift and beautiful transition to the *duties of common life:* 'I therefore, the prisoner in the Lord, beseech you to walk worthily of the calling wherewith ye were called' (4:1). . . . Finally there is a stirring call to put on the whole armor of God for the conflict with the powers of evil—a metaphor which may have been suggested to Paul by his military surroundings at Rome."—*McClymont*.

3. Read Ephesians 6:10-18.

PAUL'S SUBLIME PRAYER: Read slowly and carefully Ephesians 3:14-21, and try to realize what it meant to Paul to write those words. Pray, too, that this prayer may be laden with meaning to you as well.

Study XXII.—Paul's Last Travels, Second Imprisonment, and Death

First Day: Paul's Last Travels

Paul's first imprisonment in Rome lasted two years. During that time he wrote the four epistles recently studied: *Philippians, Colossians, Philemon,* and *Ephesians*. From the three epistles which yet remain for study—*First Timothy, Titus,* and *Second Timothy*—it is possible to learn something about Paul's last travels and about his second imprisonment that ended in his death.

The order of the closing events in Paul's life is extremely uncertain. The arrangement given in to-day's lesson is substantially that contained in Professor Burton's *Records and Letters of the Apostolic Age,* pages 225, 226.

1. Paul expected to be released from prison and to visit Macedonia and Asia: Philippians 2:24 and Philemon 22.
2. He may have gone to Spain: St. Chrysostom (347-407 A.D.) declares that St. Paul, after his residence in Rome, departed to Spain. It was Paul's intention to visit Spain: see Romans 15:24-28.
3. He returned to the East, and visited Ephesus, where he left Timothy in charge: 1 Tim. 1:3.
4. He went into Macedonia. While there he wrote his *First Epistle to Timothy*.
5. He went from Macedonia to Asia, stopping at Troas, where he left a cloak and some books: 2 Tim. 4:13. From Troas he journeyed to Miletus, where he left Trophimus: 2 Tim. 4:20.
6. From Miletus he went to Crete, where he left Titus: Titus 1:5.
7. From Crete he went to Corinth, where he left Erastus (2 Tim. 4:20), and thence probably wrote his *Epistle to Titus*.
8. From Corinth he went to Nicopolis (Titus 3:12). Here he was arrested, and sent hence to Rome.
9. In Rome he wrote *The Second Epistle to Timothy,* and was beheaded under Nero in 65 A.D.

Study XXII.—Paul's Last Travels, Second Imprisonment, and Death

Second Day: Paul's First Epistle to Timothy

Among the places that Paul visited after his release from prison was the city of Ephesus. Here he left Timothy in charge of the Church, and departed for Macedonia. While in Macedonia the apostle wrote the letter known as *The First Epistle to Timothy*.

1. What was Timothy's native city? Who were his parents? See Acts 16:1 and 2 Timothy 1:5.
2. To whom was the conversion of Timothy due? See 1 Tim. 1:2.
3. Timothy accompanied Paul on his second and third missionary journeys. He was also with the apostle at Rome. When Paul wrote to the Philippians, he purposed to send Timothy to them. Read Philippians 2:19-22. When Paul came east from Rome, he may have found Timothy at Ephesus.
4. Paul was in Macedonia when he wrote his *First Epistle to Timothy:* 1 Tim. 1:3 and 4; he expected to revisit Ephesus in the near future: 1 Tim. 3:14 and 15, but fearing that he might be hindered, he wrote this letter of instructions to Timothy.

THE FIRST EPISTLE TO TIMOTHY

5. Paul's cares were increasing daily. The Church was growing rapidly and gaining in importance; questions of organization and of Church government were in need of settlement; false doctrines of two general classes were noticeable: Judaistic teaching concerning the Law of Moses as essential to faith; and teaching of an obscure character, involving Greek and Oriental philosophy.
6. Paul wrote this letter to inspire Timothy with a high ideal of life and conduct that he might successfully organize and administer the Church at Ephesus, and might root out heresies and elevate the moral tone of the members.
7. Exhortations addressed to Timothy:
    (a) His mission at Ephesus 1:3 and 4.
    (b) General charge to Timothy. Read 1 Tim. 1:18-20; 4:6-16; 6:6-16; and 6:20 and 21.

Memory Verse: Memorize 1 Timothy 4:12.

STUDY XXII.—**Paul's Last Travels, Second Imprisonment, and Death**

THIRD DAY: PAUL'S FIRST EPISTLE TO TIMOTHY
(CONTINUED)

Interesting details concerning the Church at Ephesus—its troubles and tendencies—are contained in Paul's letter to Timothy. Especially noteworthy is St. Paul's method of dealing with certain vexatious questions that were arising.

1. Disputes over the lifeless and useless precepts of the Jewish Law: 1 Tim. 1:5-7.
2. The forwardness of certain women in the Church: 1 Tim. 2:9-15.
3. Heresies that St. Paul foresees as likely to spring up: 1 Tim. 4:1-5.
4. In the eyes of the Gospel all men were equal; how, then, were Christian slaves to regard their masters? 1 Tim. 6:1 and 2.
5. The worldliness of certain rich Christians: 1 Tim. 6:6-10 and 17-19.

LESSON THOUGHT: When discouraged by the appearance of evils in the Church at the present time, it is well for one to remember that even in the days of the apostles there were troubles of the same kind. Human nature is the same, whether in the twentieth century or the first century. Men have the same tendency toward sin, and need the Gospel just as much now as then.

PRAYER: "O Lord, grant that my heart may be truly cleansed and filled with Thy Holy Spirit, and that I may arise to serve Thee, and lie down to sleep in entire confidence in Thee, and submission to Thy will, ready for life or for death. Let me live for this day, not overcharged with worldly cares, but feeling that my treasure is not here, and desiring truly to be joined to Thee in Thy heavenly kingdom, and to those who have already gone to Thee. O Lord, save me from sin, and guide me with Thy Spirit, and keep me in faithful obedience to Thee, through Jesus Christ Thy Son our Lord." *Amen.*

STUDY XXII.—**Paul's Last Travels, Second Imprisonment, and Death**

FOURTH DAY: PAUL'S EPISTLE TO TITUS

Paul wrote his *First Epistle to Timothy* in Macedonia. At the time of writing he hoped soon to visit Timothy at Ephesus. On leaving Macedonia Paul seems to have gone to Troas; he may then have visited Ephesus. From Ephesus he went to Miletus. Departing from Miletus he went to Crete, where he left Titus to take charge of the organization of the Cretan churches. From Crete, Paul went to Corinth, and while there wrote *The Epistle to Titus*.
1. Paul at Troas: 2 Tim. 4:13; at Ephesus (?): 1 Tim. 3:14; at Miletus: 2 Tim. 4:20; Crete: Titus 1:5; Corinth: 2 Tim. 4:20.
2. Titus was a Greek (Gal. 2:3), and was one of Paul's converts (Titus 1:4). He accompanied Paul to Jerusalem to the conference concerning the status of Gentiles in the Church (Study XI). Paul also entrusted him with important commissions to the Corinthian Church; he now leaves him in charge of the Church in Crete, and writes a letter to him similar to the letter sent to Timothy. Tradition affirms that Titus was the first bishop of Crete.

THE EPISTLE TO TITUS

3. It is uncertain when the Cretan Church was established. Cretans were in Jerusalem on the Day of Pentecost (Acts 2:11). Paul may have visited the island during his sojourn of two years at Corinth. Mark Crete with a cross on your map.
4. For what purpose was Titus left in Crete? Titus 1:5.
5. The Cretans did not have a good reputation:
    (a) They were notorious for lying: See Titus 1:12. From what poet is this quotation taken? See page 16. In ancient times "to Cretize" was *to lie*.
    (b) They were unruly and talkative: Titus 1:10 and 11.
    (c) They were guilty of impurity: Titus 1:15 and 16.
6. Brief outline of the contents of the letter:
    (a) Qualifications of Church officers: 1:5-9.
    (b) The conduct of Church members: 2:1-10.
    (c) Instructions of a general nature: 3:1-11.

LESSON THOUGHT: In the closing lines of this letter are found these words (verse 14), "and let our *people* also learn to maintain good works for necessary uses, that they be not unfruitful." What does Paul mean by "our people"? Do these words apply to us as Christians? In what way to-day shall you maintain "good works for necessary uses" so as to be not unfruitful?

Study XXII.—**Paul's Last Travels, Second Imprisonment, and Death**

FIFTH DAY: PAUL'S ARREST AND SECOND IMPRISONMENT AT ROME

After writing his *Epistle to Titus,* Paul left Corinth, and went to Nicopolis. He was probably arrested there, and taken thence to Rome. Interesting glimpses of the apostle are contained in his *Second Epistle to Timothy.*

1. Paul's movements:
    (a) He left Erastus at Corinth: 2 Tim. 4:20.
    (b) His intention of going to Nicopolis: Titus 3:12.
    (c) Nicopolis (*city of victory*), in Epirus, was founded by Augustus in 31 B.C. to commemorate his victory at Actium. It was a good center for missionary work in Epirus, Illyricum, and Dalmatia. Mark Nicopolis with a cross on your outline map.
    (d) How much time did Paul plan to spend in Nicopolis? Titus 3:12.
2. The cause of Paul's arrest:
    (a) It was now the year 67 A.D. Three years before this time Rome had been burned, and the Christians were accused of having set it on fire. At once a most cruel persecution broke out against them.
    (b) So prominent a Christian leader as Paul was a great prize for capture. Probably some Roman officer, wishing to please the Emperor, seized Paul and sent him to Rome.
3. The character of Paul's second imprisonment:
    (a) Owing to persecution, the Christians of Rome had been killed or driven into hiding. Paul no longer had their presence and help.
    (b) Paul was in need of help and sympathy. Who "refreshed" him at this time? 2 Tim. 1:16-18.
    (c) His friends were absent or else had forsaken him: 2 Tim. 4:10.
    (d) Who alone was with him? 2 Tim. 4:11 (first clause).
    (e) No longer in his own hired house, he sends a thousand miles for his cloak and his books: 2 Tim. 4:13.

PAUL'S CONFIDENCE: Was Paul discouraged, and did he lose confidence in the Lord? Read 2 Tim. 1:8-12, dwelling with particular thought upon verse 12.

STUDY XXII.—**Paul's Last Travels, Second Imprisonment, and Death**

SIXTH DAY: PAUL'S SECOND EPISTLE TO TIMOTHY

Paul's life was now drawing to a close. He was in prison, anticipating a speedy sentence of death. Longing for Timothy, he writes urging him to come to Rome. This letter, known as *The Second Epistle to Timothy*, is a precious possession: it gives us glimpses of Paul's final imprisonment (studied yesterday); it reveals Paul's affection for Timothy; it contains much useful advice and exhortation; and, lastly, it preserves what are practically the last words of the apostle.

1. Where had Timothy been left by Paul, and for what purpose?
2. Paul's longing for Timothy: 2 Tim. 1:4.
3. Who alone was with Paul at this time?
4. Paul urges Timothy to come to him: 2 Tim. 4:9 and 11.
5. Why does Paul say in 2 Tim. 4:11 that Mark is "profitable for the ministry"? See Acts 15:37 and 38. Does it not appear that Paul was anxious to commend and reinstate Mark?
6. Paul evidently fears that Timothy may not be able to reach Rome in time to see him before his execution; he gives final advice and instruction to Timothy:
    (a) He must be true to his teaching: 2 Tim. 1:13, 14, and 3:14-17.
    (b) Like a soldier, he must attend strictly to his duties; like an athlete in the games, he must contend lawfully: 2 Tim. 2:1-5.
    (c) He must be pure and gentle: 2 Tim. 2:22-25.
7. Paul warns Timothy of certain dangers within the Church:
    (a) The wickedness of evil men: 2 Tim. 3:1-5.
    (b) The danger of false doctrine: 2 Tim. 4:1-4.

MEMORY VERSES: Memorize 2 Tim. 3:16 and 17—verses which are particularly applicable to this last Epistle of St. Paul.

STUDY XXII.—**Paul's Last Travels, Second Imprisonment, and Death**

SEVENTH DAY: THE DEATH OF ST. PAUL

Tradition asserts that Paul was beheaded at Rome outside the city walls at a point on the road to Ostia. The year of his death may be given as 65 A.D., toward the end of the reign of Nero.

1. At the first trial or hearing, Paul seems to have had no one to support him; he prayed for those who deserted him: 2 Tim. 4:16.
2. How did Paul evidently make use of the opportunity of speaking that was given him at the trial? 2 Tim. 4:17.
3. What does he mean in 2 Tim. 4:17 (end of the verse) by the words, "I was delivered out of the mouth of the lion"?
4. What was Paul's hope and confidence? 2 Tim. 4:18.
5. The second (and last) trial probably took place shortly after the first. This time Paul's accusers succeeded in securing his condemnation.
6. *Paul's last words:* Three verses of Second Timothy may be regarded in content and in spirit as practically Paul's last words: Read 2 Tim. 4:6-8.

"The trial ended, Paul was condemned and delivered over to the executioner. He was led out of the city with a crowd of the lowest rabble at his heels. The fatal spot was reached: he knelt beside the block; the headsman's axe gleamed in the sun and fell; and the head of the apostle of the world rolled in the dust. . . .

"Yet Paul lives among us to-day with a life a hundredfold more influential than that which throbbed in his brain while the earthly hull which made him visible still lingered on earth. Wherever the feet of them who publish the glad tidings go forth beautiful upon the mountains, he walks by their side as an inspirer and a guide; in ten thousand churches every Sabbath, and on a thousand hearths every day, his eloquent lips still teach that gospel of which he was never ashamed; and wherever there are human souls searching for the white flower of holiness, or climbing the difficult height of self-denial, there he whose life was so pure, whose devotion to Christ was so entire, and whose pursuit of a single purpose was so unceasing, is welcomed as the best of friends."—*Stalker.*

PART IX

The Personality and Service of Paul

Study XXIII.—Personal Characteristics of St. Paul
Study XXIV.—Paul's Services to the World

Study XXIII.—**Personal Characteristics of St. Paul**
First Day: Paul's Personal Appearance

Testimony regarding the personal appearance of St. Paul is extremely scanty. Only two passages in the New Testament yield any information on this point, and both of them are tantalizing in their brevity. In the works of later writers, however, from the third to the fifteenth century A.D., are found certain traditional accounts of the appearance of the apostle. Though these accounts are too late to be entirely trustworthy, nevertheless they agree in certain important respects.

1. Read Acts 14:11 and 12. In your previous study of these verses to what conclusion did you come regarding the stature and appearance of Paul? See also page 76, section 4.
2. In his *Second Epistle to the Corinthians,* Paul quotes certain criticisms which his enemies had made about his speech and presence: See 2 Cor. 10:10.
3. In a romance of the third century entitled *The Acts of Paul and Thekla,* Paul is described as "short, with meeting eyebrows, hook-nosed, full of grace."
4. John of Antioch (sixth century) says that "Paul was, in person, round-shouldered, with a sprinkling of gray on his head and beard, with an aquiline nose, grayish eyes, meeting eyebrows, with a mixture of pale and red in his complexion, and an ample beard. With a genial expression of countenance, he was sensible, earnest, easily accessible, sweet and inspired with the Holy Spirit."
5. Nicephorus (fifteenth century) writes that "Paul was short and dwarfish in stature, and, as it were, crooked in person and slightly bent. His face was pale, his aspect winning. He was baldheaded, and his eyes were bright. His nose was prominent and aquiline, his beard thick and tolerably long, and both this and his head were sprinkled with white hairs."
6. Read again carefully the testimony of the writers given above in sections 3 to 5, noticing particularly their points of agreement. Let your imagination create a picture of the apostle.

The Beauty of Holiness: The scattered fragments of ancient testimony agree in stating that Paul had a pleasant and winning expression of countenance. Paul was *reflecting Christ:* "But we all, with unveiled face, reflecting, as a mirror, the glory of the Lord, are transformed into the same image from glory to glory."—*Second Corinthians* 3:18 (R.V.).

STUDY XXIII.—**Personal Characteristics of St. Paul**
SECOND DAY: PAUL'S "THORN IN THE FLESH"

Paul was troubled with a certain infirmity or weakness of body, which he calls his "thorn in the flesh." This may have had some influence upon his personal appearance and bearing.

1. Read 2 Corinthians 12:1-10.
2. According to Paul's own statement, why was the "thorn in the flesh" given to him?
3. Why does Paul glory in this weakness?
4. Paul seems to have had an attack of this mysterious malady on the occasion of his first visit among the Galatians: See Galatians 4:13 and 14.
5. It is impossible to determine what Paul's thorn in the flesh really was. It was a weakness of body that afflicted him from time to time; it was extremely painful; it humiliated him, and made him an object of contempt; and in its workings it was mysterious and apparently of diabolical origin (2 Cor. 12:7). Scholars have proposed various theories regarding Paul's weakness: some think he was troubled with acute *ophthalmia*—an inflammation of the eyes—and cite Gal. 4:15 as evidence; others suggest certain forms of *hysteria* or *epilepsy;* a recent view is that he was subject to malarial fever. Perhaps the most satisfactory theory is the suggestion that he had epileptic seizures. His thorn in the flesh afflicted him directly after his ecstatic vision (2 Cor. 12:1-6), and may have been due to an overwrought condition of his nervous system. For slight additional evidence see 2 Cor. 5:13 and Acts 26:24.
6. Notwithstanding this peculiar ailment which distressed him at times, Paul must have had a vigorous constitution. If he had not, he never could have endured the many hardships and trials that fell to his lot as he preached the Gospel throughout the heathen world.

MEMORY VERSE: Memorize 2 Cor. 12:9.

Study XXIII.—**Personal Characteristics of St. Paul**
Third Day: Paul a Man of Courage, Activity, and Enthusiasm

Paul was a man of courage, activity, and enthusiasm. Not only was he courageous in the face of danger, but also he dared to maintain an unpopular cause in the presence of those whom men would naturally wish to conciliate; he displayed great activity in his preaching and teaching, and showed the highest enthusiasm in all his work.

1. Paul's *Courage:*
   (a) What incident showed Paul's courage at Ephesus? See Acts 19:29 and 30.
   (b) Read the catalogue of some of the hardships, perils, and sufferings which Paul experienced: 2 Cor. 11:23-27.
   (c) Paul's courage of conviction: Gal. 2:11-14. Why did it take especial courage to criticise Peter?
2. Paul's *Activity:*
   (a) The record of Paul's missionary journeys, filled with incessant toils and labors, testifies abundantly to the activity of the apostle.
   (b) The keen physical activity of the Greek athletic games interested him greatly; he often likens himself to a contestant: Gal. 2:2; 1 Cor. 9:26 and 27; 2 Tim. 4:7 and 8.
3. Paul's *Enthusiasm:*
   (a) Paul's enthusiasm is most plainly seen in his letters. In his eagerness and earnestness he is at times almost incoherent; the line of thought is not always easy to follow; there are abrupt transitions and puzzling omissions.
   (b) Paul, as he writes, is at times swept off his feet, so to speak, by a rush of feeling. On such occasions he bursts out in a doxology or in pious ejaculations in the praise of God: See Romans 11:33-36.
   (c) Paul seems at times, at least, to have spoken rapidly and with great feeling: Acts 26:24, and 2 Cor. 5:13.

Prayer: "Give us courage, Lord, to do always that which is pleasing to Thee; grant that we may be diligent and active in Thy service, running with patience the race that is set before us; and fill us with joy and enthusiasm that we may labor heartily and cheerfully in spreading Thy kingdom in the hearts of men."—*Amen.*

Study XXIII.—Personal Characteristics of St. Paul
Fourth Day: Paul a Happy Man

Paul, in spite of his thorn in the flesh, and in spite of his excessive labor and suffering for the Gospel, was a happy man. Not only was he happy himself, but he also wished others to be happy.

1. Paul's Epistles abound in verses in which his happiness is openly expressed:
    (a) Paul's converts were a source of great happiness to him: See 1 Thess. 2:19 and 20; 2 Cor. 7:7, 9, and 16; Philippians 1:4; 2:2, 16 and 17; 4:1.
    (b) Another source of happiness was the spread of the Gospel: See Philippians 1:18.
    (c) Even his sufferings for the sake of the Gospel were a source of joy to him: 2 Cor. 7:4; 12:10; and Colossians 1:24.
2. Paul wished his converts to be happy: See 1 Thess. 5:16; and Philippians 4:4.
3. The real secret of Paul's happiness was the abiding presence of the Holy Spirit; this happiness was always his, and was independent of external conditions; hence, even when troubled on every side, his well-spring of joy never failed:
    (a) The presence of the Holy Spirit a source of joy: See 1 Thess. 1:6; Romans 14:17.
    (b) The Holy Spirit is a source of peace and joy because it makes men feel the love of God: Romans 5:1-5.

THE LOVE OF GOD: Paul was secure in the possession of his happiness that came from the love of God. Let him speak for himself: "I am persuaded that neither death, nor life, nor angels, nor principalities, nor powers, nor things present, nor things to come, nor height, nor depth, nor any other creature, shall be able to separate us from the love of God, which is in Christ Jesus our Lord."—*Epistle to the Romans* 8:38 and 39.

Study XXIII.—Personal Characteristics of St. Paul
Fifth Day: Paul a Man Who Loved Men

Paul was successful in his labors among men because he loved them. He was a man of friendships: he loved his friends, and they returned his affection. Because he loved men, he avoided saying and doing those things which would unnecessarily offend or wound them, hence he was a man of tact, courtesy, and adaptability.

1. Paul speaks of his friends with the greatest affection; he never traveled alone, but always had one or more of his friends with him.
    (a) Among the many friends of Paul mentioned in Acts and in the Epistles, two deserve special notice: Luke and Timothy. Both traveled with him, and both were with him when in prison.
    (b) Luke: In what way does Paul speak of Luke in Col. 4:14? Where was Paul when he wrote *Colossians?*
    (c) Timothy: Paul's affection for Timothy is clearly expressed in 2 Tim. 1:2-4. See also 1 Cor. 4:17.
2. Paul's friends and converts returned his affection: See Acts 20:36-38; 21:4 and 5. Luke's affection for Paul may be learned from 2 Tim. 4:11 (first sentence). Where was Paul when he wrote *Second Timothy?* What were the circumstances under which it was written?
3. Paul's tact: The apostle was tactful in approaching and dealing with men:
    (a) How was this quality shown in the opening words of his address at Athens, Acts 17:22-24? See page 103, section 8.
    (b) How was it shown also in his address before Felix, Acts 24:10? In his address before Agrippa, Acts 26:1-3?
    (c) Paul's *Epistle to Philemon* is a most tactful letter. What were the circumstances under which it was written?
4. Paul's adaptability: Paul's love for humanity and his ready sympathy enabled him to adapt himself to all sorts and conditions of men: See 1 Cor. 9:19-23.

Love "the Greatest Thing in the World": In the thirteenth chapter of *First Corinthians* Paul writes on "Love." Henry Drummond tells of a man who read this chapter once a week for three months, and it changed his life. Read this chapter and then read at your earliest opportunity Drummond's essay on it entitled: *The Greatest Thing in the World.*

Study XXIII.—Personal Characteristics of St. Paul
Sixth Day: Paul a Man of Prayer

Paul was a man of prayer. He prayed earnestly for his converts, and asked them to pray for him. In his Epistles he gave many directions concerning prayer. From one sublime prayer preserved in *The Epistle to the Ephesians* it is possible to learn about the character of Paul's prayers.

1. Luke, in the book of Acts, mentions several occasions when Paul had recourse to prayer: At Philippi, Acts 16:25; at Miletus, 20:36; at Tyre, 21:5; at Jerusalem, 22:17; on the island of Melita, 28:8.
2. Paul prayed for his converts and for the churches to which they belonged:
    (a) The Thessalonians: 1 Thess. 1:2; 2 Thess. 1:11.
    (b) The Corinthians: 2 Cor. 13:7.
    (c) The Romans: Rom. 1:9 and 10.
    (d) The Philippians: Phil. 1:3 and 4.
    (e) The Colossians: Col. 1:3 and 9.
    (f) The Ephesians: Eph. 1:16.
    (g) Philemon: Philem. 4.
    (h) Timothy: 2 Tim. 1:3.
3. Paul asked his converts to pray for him:
    (a) 2 Thess. 3:1; Philippians 1:19; Ephesians 6:18 and 19; Col. 4:3 and 4.
    (b) For what end does Paul request these prayers?
4. He gave, also, certain directions concerning prayer. See 1 Thess. 5:17; 1 Tim. 2:1, 2, and 8; Philippians 4:6.
5. Paul's sublime prayer: Read Ephesians 3:14-21.

Thought for To-day: Paul gave much time to earnest prayer. Do you pray every day, or do you sometimes forget to talk with God? Do you pray only at night, just before you go to bed, when you are often too tired to know clearly what you are saying? Do you pray for others, as Paul did, or do you pray only for yourself? Will you not resolve to be more thoughtful and earnest in your prayers?

Study XXIII.—Personal Characteristics of St. Paul
Seventh Day: Paul's Devotion to Christ

"Paul's personal devotion to Christ was the supreme characteristic of the man, and from first to last the mainspring of his activities. From the moment of his first meeting with Christ he had but one passion; his love for his Saviour burned with more and more brightness to the end. He delighted to call himself the slave of Christ, and had no ambition except to be the propagator of His ideas and the continuer of His influence."—*Stalker.*

1. In the first verse of three of his Epistles, Paul calls himself a "servant of Jesus Christ" (*Romans, Philippians,* and *Titus*). The word rendered here as *servant* means, rather, *slave*; and, moreover, one who is a slave by birth. See also Acts 27:23.
2. His one aim was to spread the Gospel of Christ: 1 Cor. 2:2 and 9:16; Philippians 1:14-18.
3. He earnestly desired that Christ should be magnified in his body: Philippians 1:20.
4. He says that he was continuing the work of Christ and was filling up what was lacking in His sufferings: Col. 1:24.
5. He bore the marks of the Lord Jesus in his body: Gal. 6:17.
6. Christ was his life: Philippians 1:21-23.

"Paul had the sense that Christ had done everything for him; He had entered into him, casting out the old Paul and ending the old life, and had begotten a new man, with new designs, feelings, and activities. And it was his deepest longing that this process should go on and become complete—that his old self should vanish quite away, and that the new self, which Christ had created in His own image, and still sustained, should become so predominant that, when the thoughts of his mind were Christ's thoughts, the words on his lips Christ's words, the deeds he did Christ's deeds, and the character he wore Christ's character, he might be able to say, 'I live; yet not I, but Christ liveth in me.'"—*Stalker.*

STUDY XXIV.—**Paul's Services to the World**

FIRST DAY: PAUL A WORLD-MISSIONARY

In summing up the services of St. Paul, it is first of all necessary to note that he preached the Gospel to practically the whole world of his day.

1. The world, in St. Paul's time, was very much smaller than it is to-day. It comprised chiefly those lands that were under Roman rule—the lands bordering on the Mediterranean.
2. What was Paul's commission as a world-missionary? See Acts 9:15.
3. It was Paul's practice, in spreading the Gospel, to go to the capital, or most important city, of each province of the Roman Empire, and from that center to labor in the surrounding region. What important city was the headquarters of his work in Syria? In the Roman province of Asia? In Macedonia? In Achaia?
4. Paul's work was done thoroughly:
    (a) What does Luke say of his work in the province of Asia? Acts 19:20 and 26.
    (b) Before Paul was taken to Rome he had preached the Gospel in all the lands of the Eastern Mediterranean: Romans 15:19 and 23.
    (c) While a prisoner at Rome, he made converts in the household of Cæsar and in the Prætorian guard: Philippians 4:22 and 1:12-14 (R.V.).
    (d) Paul's plan for the evangelizing of the world took in Spain: See Romans 15:24. Certain early Christian writers affirm that he preached and labored there: See page 170, section 2.
5. Yet Paul did not preach in all parts of the Roman Empire. There is no evidence in the New Testament to show that he visited Britain, Gaul, or Egypt. The Roman conquest of Britain did not really begin until 43 A.D., hence in Paul's time the Britons were still uncivilized; on the other hand, Gaul was being rapidly Romanized, and Egypt was a seat of culture. What reason does Paul give for not preaching in certain regions? See Romans 15:20.

LESSON THOUGHT: Paul, in his life-work, fulfilled literally the promise and prophecy made by Christ on Ascension Day: Acts 1:8.

STUDY XXIV.—**Paul's Services to the World**

SECOND DAY: PAUL THE INTERPRETER OF CHRISTIANITY

The world of St. Paul's time was the Roman Empire. It was dominated, however, by the Greek language and by Greek habits of thought. Though the Romans had conquered Greece, yet Greek art, literature, and philosophy mastered the Romans. The Greek mind was quick, alert, eager, and questioning. To the world of his day, permeated with Greek thought, Paul interpreted the life, death, and teachings of Christ.

1. Alexander the Great, before his death, in 323 B.C., had conquered the world. He wished to make the world a Greek world, consequently he planted colonies throughout his vast empire, and encouraged the spread of the Greek language and culture. So thoroughly was the work done that even after his empire had passed into the hands of the Romans it kept its character as a Greek Empire; the Greek language became well-nigh a universal language.
2. The Greek philosophers had groped after God. But with all their wisdom they had failed to find Him. They were dissatisfied with paganism, and longed for a purer and better religion that should uplift and ennoble them.
3. While the world was waiting for a deliverer, Jesus was born in the obscure province of Judea. His public ministry lasted three years, 27-30 A.D. He was a Jew, and His teachings were given in that form which was most expressive to Jews. Who was to interpret His life, death, and resurrection to the Gentile world? Who was to explain the philosophy of the plan of salvation to a world well trained in argument, discussion, and debate?
4. How was Paul especially fitted by birth and training to preach to the Greek world?
5. What does Paul himself say of the Greek mind? 1 Cor. 1:22.
6. Paul taught that the Gospel was a higher form of knowledge than the philosophic *wisdom* of the Greeks: 1 Cor. 1:17-24.

THOUGHT FOR TO-DAY: In preaching and writing to the Greek world, Paul was preaching and writing to us, for our methods of thought and point of view are essentially those of the Greeks. "We are all Greeks. Our law, our literature, our religion, our art, have their roots in Greece."—*Shelley.*

Study XXIV.—Paul's Services to the World
Third Day: Paul's Successful Combat with Judaism

In his work of spreading the Gospel about the Roman Empire, and in adapting its teachings to Greek methods of thought, Paul met his greatest opposition among the Jews. Moreover, the most dangerous opposition was not that of the unbelieving Jews, but that of the Jewish party within the Church, which tried to impose the Mosaic Law on all Gentile converts. That Christianity did not become a sect of Judaism is due to the vigorous work of St. Paul.

1. God chose the Jewish nation for training in religion; He revealed Himself to the patriarchs; He gave laws to Moses; and He spoke through the prophets. The religious teachers of the Jews added to the Laws of Moses (the *Written* Law) a mass of minute and intricate rules (the *Oral* Law), and imposed the whole on the Jewish people—"a yoke," said Peter, "which neither our fathers nor we were able to bear."
2. The Judaizing party within the Church tried to force the Law upon the Gentiles: For two references, selected from many, see Acts 15:1 and Galatians 3:1-3.
3. What charges did this party bring against Paul? Acts 21:20 and 21.
4. What did Paul consider to have been the true work of the Law? Galatians 3:23-28.
5. In nearly every one of his Epistles, Paul touched on the question of the relation of the Gentiles to the Law. He was pre-eminently the apostle of the Gentiles and the champion of Gentile freedom. His arguments against the Judaizing party are most fully stated in *Galatians* and *Romans*.
6. Paul was beheaded in 65 A.D. In 70 A.D., Titus captured and destroyed Jerusalem. Judaism no longer had a center for the national worship, nor could it answer the keen arguments of Paul. The apostle had won, and had established the truth of the equality of all men in the eyes of the Gospel: "Where there is neither Greek nor Jew, circumcision nor uncircumcision, Barbarian, Scythian, bond nor free: but Christ is all, and in all" (Col. 3:11).

Study XXIV.—Paul's Services to the World
Fourth Day: Paul the Organizer of the Church

Before his death, Paul foresaw that the Christian Church was in need of thorough organization to do its great work in the world, and to withstand the troubles that would assail from within and without. His last letters are filled with directions for Church organization, government, and worship.

1. What were some of the evils that Paul foresaw? See 1 Tim. 4:1-3.
2. Read also 2 Tim. 3:1-7.
3. Church organization and government:
   (a) Qualifications of a bishop, or overseer: 1 Tim. 3:1-7.
   (b) The position and dignity of elders: 1 Tim. 5:17-19. Read also Titus 1:5-9, and note that in those early days *bishop* and *elder* were synonymous terms.
   (c) Qualifications of a deacon: 1 Tim. 3:8-13.
4. Church worship:
   (a) The use of psalms and hymns: Colossians 3:16.
   (b) Prayer: 1 Tim. 2:1-3, 8.
   (c) The Lord's Supper: 1 Cor. 11:23-34.
   (d) Paul would have Church worship "edifying"; that is, it should *build up* those taking part. He would have all things done "decently and in order." See 1 Cor. 14:26 and 40.

Lesson Thought: Paul knew that there was much work to be done within the Christian Church—work requiring varied talents and endowments. Read Ephesians 4:11-13, and ask yourself what part you are willing to take in the "edifying of the body of Christ"; that is, in building up His Church.

Study XXIV.—**Paul's Services to the World**
Fifth Day: Paul's Epistles a Priceless Legacy

In the Epistles of Paul, the Christian world has a priceless legacy. Next to the four Gospels, the Epistles of St. Paul are the most important documents of the Christian Church. They expand and unfold the teaching of Christ; they contain verses and chapters that for centuries have been a help and comfort to Christians of all lands; and they reveal to us all the power, enthusiasm, love, and sympathy of the great apostle himself.

1. Even Paul's enemies admitted that his letters were powerful: See 2 Cor. 10:10.
2. Certain portions of Paul's letters are hard to understand. What did Peter say about their difficulty? 2 Peter 3:15.
3. The following table, taken, with a few hanges, from Stalker's *Life of St. Paul,* gives the chronological order of Paul's Epistles and the leading characteristic of each:

Epistle	Characteristic
1 and 2 Thessalonians	Simple beginnings. Attitude toward Christ's Second Coming
Galatians	Vehement argument against Judaizers
1 Corinthians	Picture of an apostle church
2 Corinthians	Paul's portrait of himself
Romans	Paul's gospel
Philippians	Picture of Roman imprisonment
Colossians	Paul's later gospel
Philemon	Example of Christian courtesy
Ephesians	Paul's later gospel
1 Timothy, and Titus	Form of the church
2 Timothy	The last scenes

4. Study this table carefully, and fix in mind the chronological order and characteristics of Paul's letters. His writings should always be read in their chronological order, for he was ever "getting deeper and deeper in his subject."
5. *The Epistle to the Hebrews* has been omitted from the table, because it was probably not written by Paul.

Paul's Portrait: "Paul is constantly visible in his letters. You can feel his heart throbbing in every chapter he ever wrote. He has painted his own portrait—not only that of the outward man, but his innermost feelings—as no one else could have painted it."—*Stalker.*

Study XXIV.—Paul's Services to the World
Sixth Day: Review of Study XXIII

To-day's lesson is a review of Study XXIII, *The Personal Characteristics of St. Paul* (pp. 179-185).

1. What was the personal appearance of St. Paul, according to the testimony of tradition? Does the New Testament say anything about his personal appearance?
2. What was Paul's "thorn in the flesh"? How did he turn this affliction into a blessing?
3. What evidence can you produce to show that Paul was a man of courage, activity, and enthusiasm?
4. Was Paul a happy man? What was the secret of his happiness?
5. What was the secret of Paul's influence with men?
6. What proof is there that Paul was a man of prayer?
7. Paul was a man whose supreme characteristic was personal devotion to Christ. How was this devotion shown?
8. What characteristic of St. Paul's has most impressed you during your study of his life? Has your own life been influenced at all by that of the great apostle? Have you resolved that you will cultivate some of those qualities that made him a great and effective Christian?

STUDY XXIV.—Paul's Services to the World

SEVENTH DAY: REVIEW OF STUDY XXIV

To-day's lesson is a review of Study XXIV, *St. Paul's Services to the World* (pp. 186-190).

1. In what part of the ancient world did Paul preach? Did he fail to visit any important divisions of the Roman Empire? If so, what was the reason?
2. In what way was Paul the interpreter of Christianity to the world?
3. Why was Paul compelled to combat Judaism? Was he successful?
4. What did Paul do to organize and strengthen the Christian Church?
5. How many of Paul's Epistles are extant? Why do these Epistles constitute one of the great legacies of the Christian world?
6. What feature of Paul's work has most interested you?
7. You have now reached the end of these *Studies in the Life of St. Paul*. You have been in daily contact for twenty-four weeks with the great apostle to the nations. You may not be a great missionary like Paul. In fact, you will probably not be a missionary at all in the technical sense of the word, but, like Paul, you can interpret Christ to the world by living His teachings. You may never fight an opposing sect as Paul fought Judaism, but you will find that the Church has foes to-day who are just as untiring and determined as those of the days of the apostle. You may never write great epistles that will be precious documents of the Church, but you can be a "living epistle," as says St. Paul, "known and read of all men." And remember always that Paul was a great Christian because he tried to live as Christ lived. Imitate Christ, not Paul, but let Paul's life be an encouragement to you, a proof of what man can be when he lives the life of Christ.

PAUL'S DOXOLOGY: "Now unto Him that is able to do exceeding abundantly above all that we ask or think, according to the power that worketh in us, unto Him be glory in the church by Jesus Christ throughout all ages, world without end. Amen."—*Ephesians* 3:20 and 21.

BIBLE STUDY COURSES

INTRODUCTORY

Introduction to Bible Study. *J. W. Cook.* Cloth, 25 cents; paper, 15 cents.

An elementary course, replacing "Studies in Faith and Conduct" by the same author. It deals with the authorship of the Bible, its general contents, geography, institutions and fundamental teachings.

Outline Studies in Biblical Facts and History. *I. N. De Puy and J. B. Travis.* Cloth, 35 cents; paper, 20 cents.

The four parts treat of: I. Bible Composition and History, four lessons; II. Historical Studies in the Old Testament, thirteen lessons; III. Historical Studies in the New Testament, seven lessons; IV. Conclusion, two lessons.

Progressive Bible Studies. *F. S. Goodman.* Cloth, 25 cents; paper, 15 cents.

This course is elementary in character. It contains nine lessons on the Bible and its use, nine on fundamental truths as a preparation for service and seven personal work studies in the Life of Jesus Christ.

TRAINING

Teaching of Bible Classes. *E. F. See.* Cloth, 60 cents; paper, 40 cents.

A revised and greatly enlarged edition of Mr. See's course on teacher training. The purpose of the book is to make a simple statement of the elementary principles of teaching in so far as they are applicable to Biblical instruction. The different parts are devoted to a consideration of the teacher, the student and the lesson.

Studies for Personal Workers. *H. A. Johnston.* Cloth, 66 cents; paper, 45 cents. Special abridged edition, paper, 25 cents.

Studies covering the principal features of personal work and designed to help those engaged in individual effort in winning men. Among the topics are: Man's Need, Man's Responsibility for Man, Equipment for Personal Work, Ways of Working, the Use of the Bible, and three lessons on notable personal workers.

Christ Among Men. *James McConaughy.* Cloth, 40 cents; paper, 25 cents.

A series of twenty-five lessons on Christ's interviews with individuals. This course aims to help persons in the work of winning other lives to the service of Christ and for stimulus, guidance and training for personal work.

ASSOCIATION PRESS, 124 East 28th Street, New York

BIBLE STUDY COURSES

ADVANCED

Studies in the Life of Jesus Christ. *E. I. Bosworth.* Cloth, 90 cents; paper, 60 cents.
    Detailed studies in the Gospels of Mark and John, with general surveys of the Gospels of Matthew and Luke.

Studies in the Life of Christ. *H. B. Sharman.*
    Based on "A Harmony of the Gospels," by Stevens and Burton, and arranged for daily study. Studies with Harmony in cloth, $1.25. Studies with Harmony in paper, 75 cents. Studies in cloth, 75 cents. Harmony in cloth, $1.00. The books in paper not sold separately.

Studies in the Life of Jesus. *W. H. Sallmon.* Cloth, 40 cents; paper, 25 cents.
    Outlines in twenty-five lessons for a historical study of Christ's life with emphasis upon His character as a living reality.

New Studies in Acts. *E. I. Bosworth.*
    Nineteen studies replacing Studies in Acts and Epistles, and the Records and Letters. The course has been re-written, and the study of the Epistles largely omitted. Cloth, 75 cents; paper, 50 cents.

Studies in the Life of Paul. *W. H. Sallmon.* Cloth, 40 cents: paper, 25 cents.
    Twenty-four lessons emphasizing the personality of the great apostle, dealing with his characteristics as a student, missionary, hero, etc.

Studies in Old Testament Characters. *W. W. White.* Cloth, 90 cents; paper, 60 cents.
    A revised edition of this standard book, based on the same outline, but requiring less work of the student than the previous edition.

Leaders of Israel. *G. L. Robinson.* Cloth, 75 cents; paper, 50 cents.
    Twenty-five studies portraying the character of Israel's leaders and the history of the chosen people from the time of Abraham to Christ.

Work and Teaching of the Earlier Prophets. *C. F. Kent and R. S. Smith.* Cloth, 60 cents; paper, 40 cents.
    These studies provide work for thirteen weeks and furnish especially illuminating material upon the character and work of the prophets.

Studies in the Teaching of Jesus and His Apostles. *E. I. Bosworth.* Cloth, 75 cents; paper, 50 cents.
    A stimulating topical course on New Testament teachings.

The Truth of the Apostolic Gospel. *R. A. Falconer.* Cloth, 75 cents; paper, 50 cents.
    The studies will be found very helpful to the understanding of and believing in the Gospel messages of the New Testament.

Social Teachings of Jesus. *J. W. Jenks.* Cloth, 75 cents; paper, 50 cents.
    A twelve-weeks' course of Bible study, considering the Man Jesus' attitude toward the leading social questions of today.

ASSOCIATION PRESS, 124 East 28th Street, New York